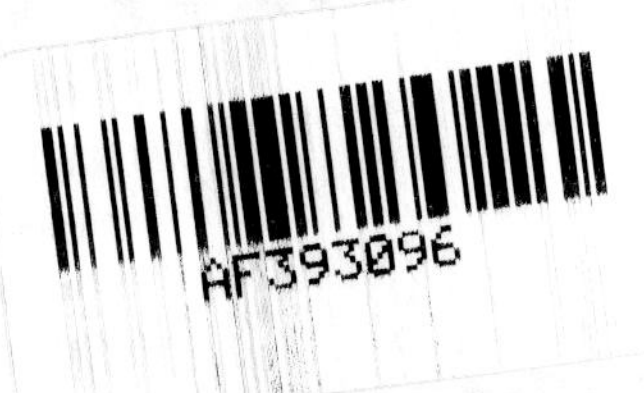

# COLORING PAGES

# PRINCESSES

## Graph Paper Team

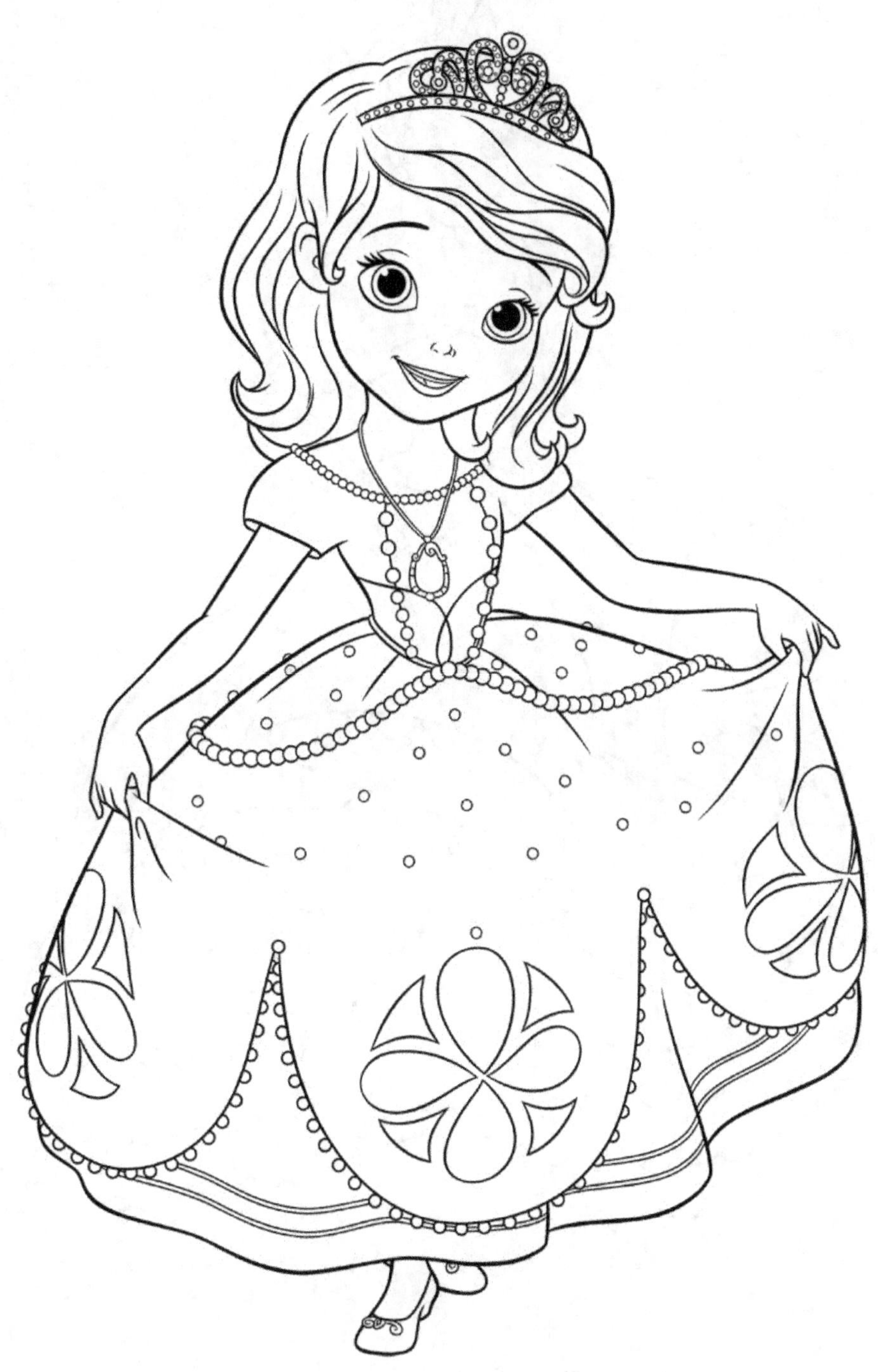

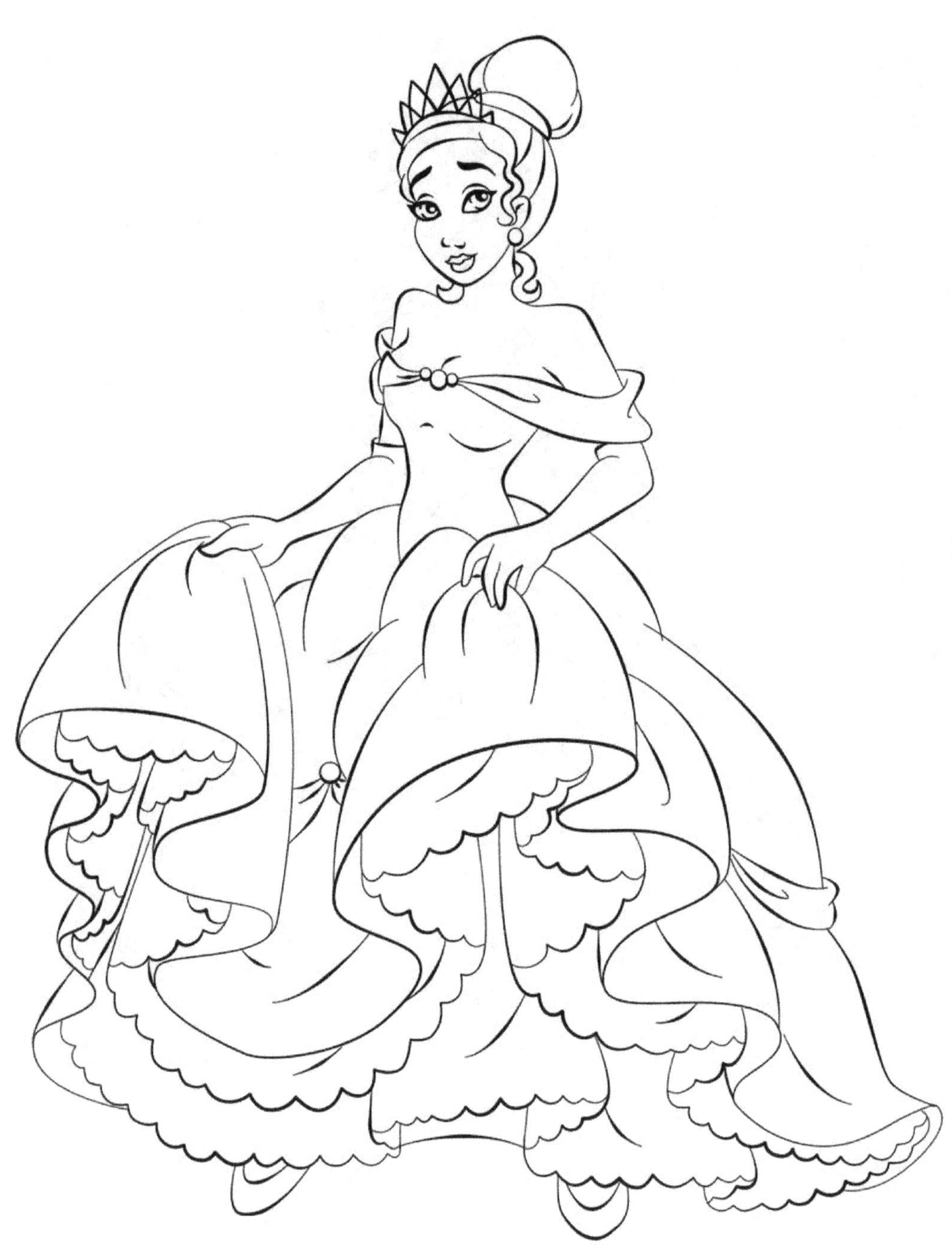

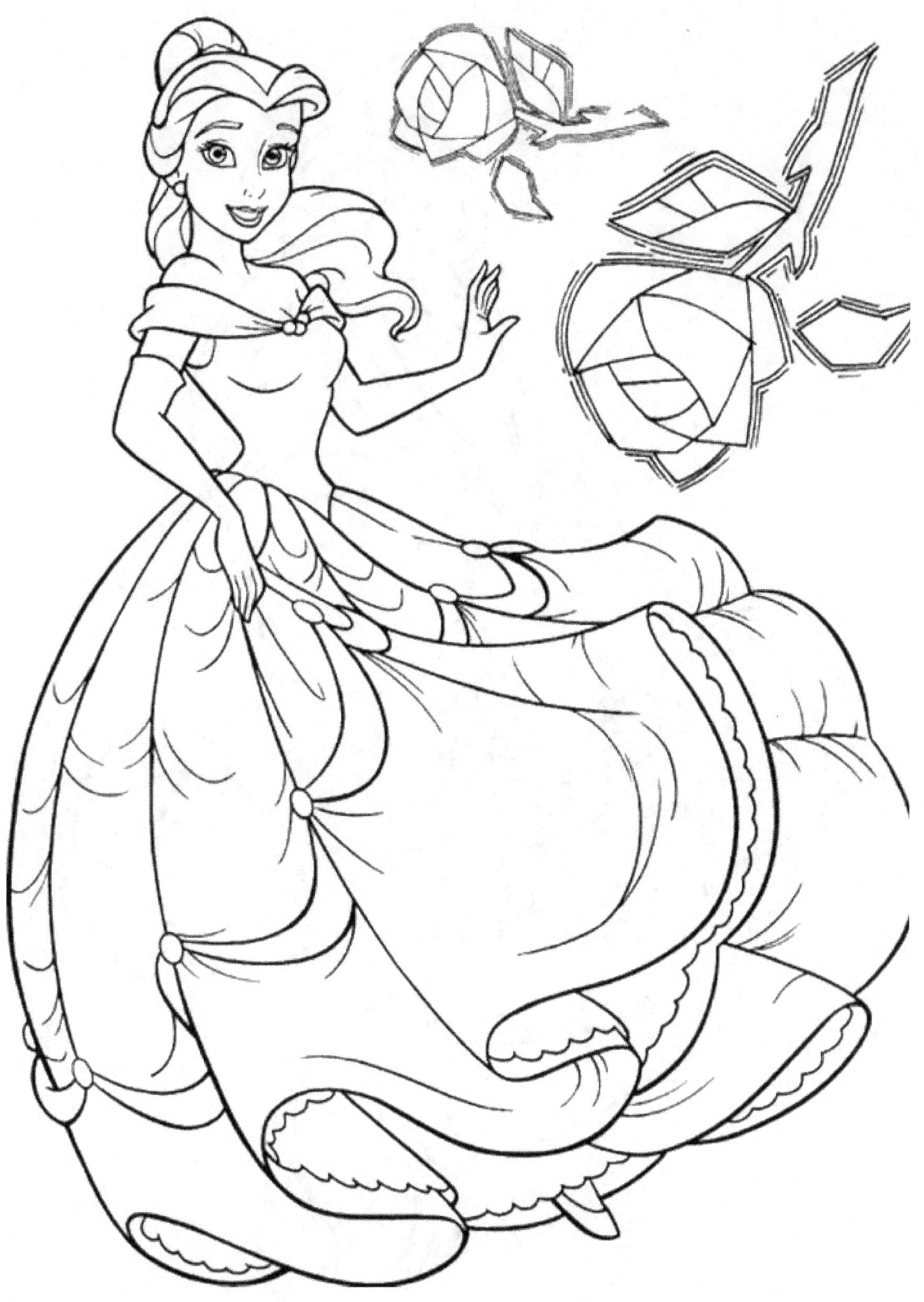

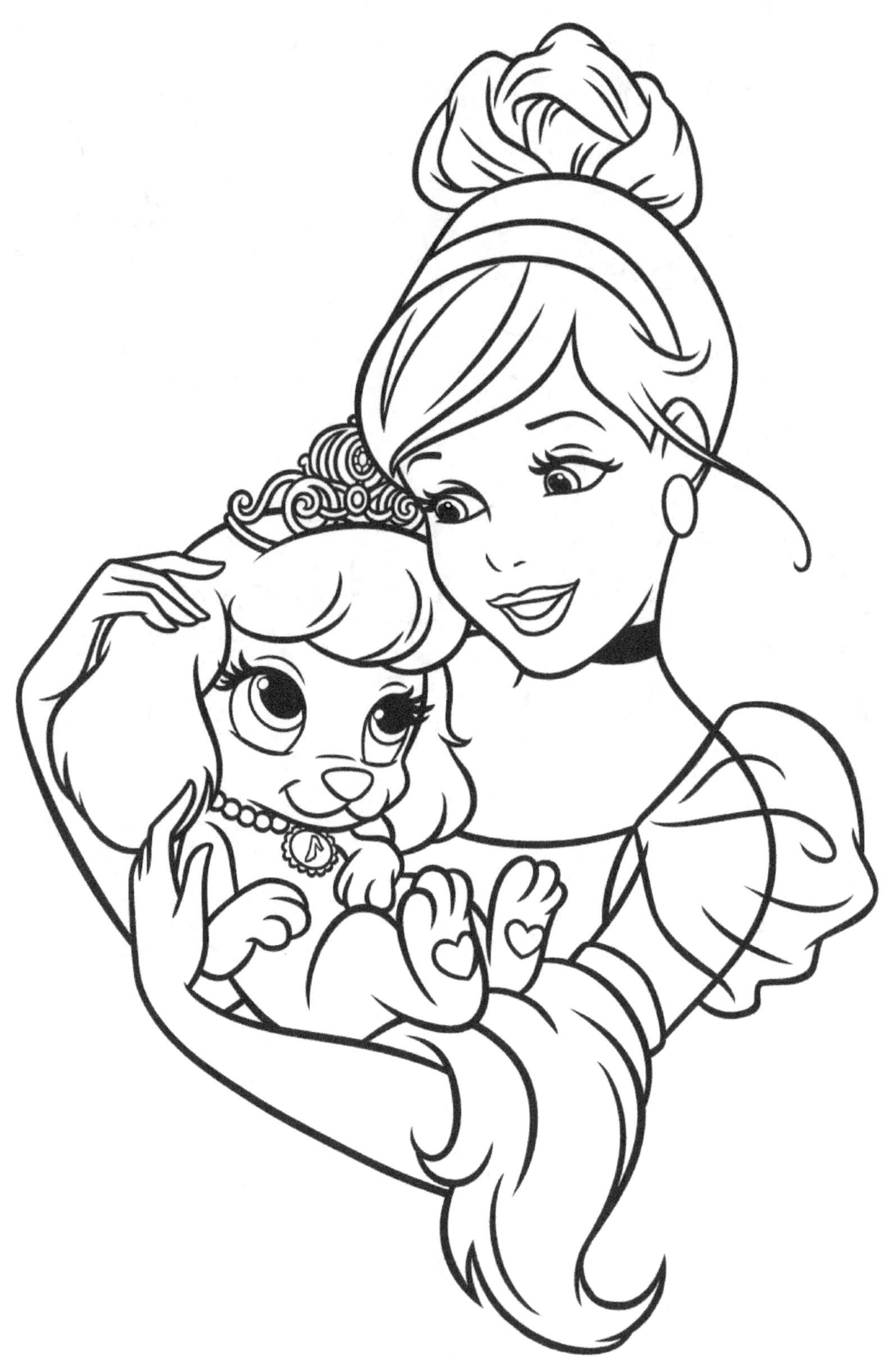

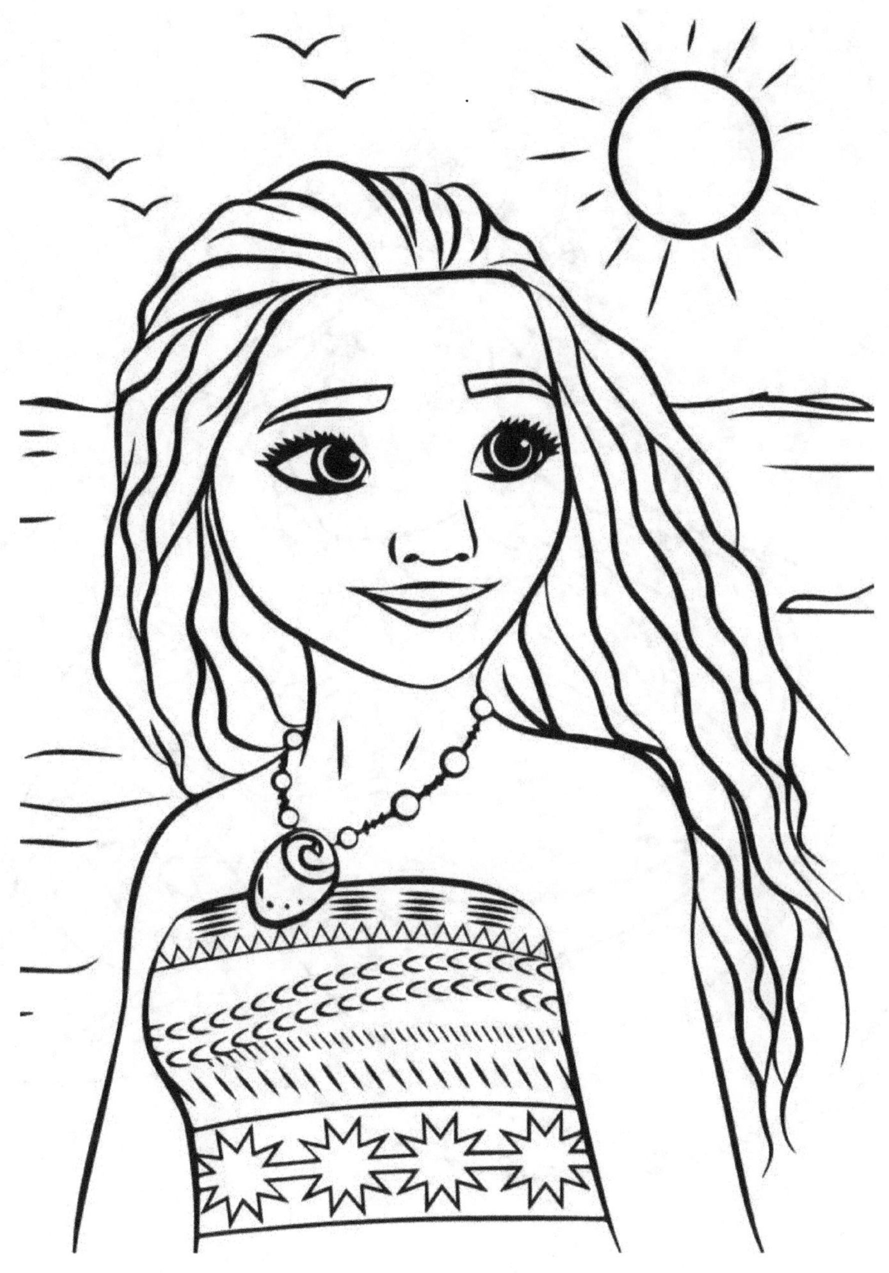

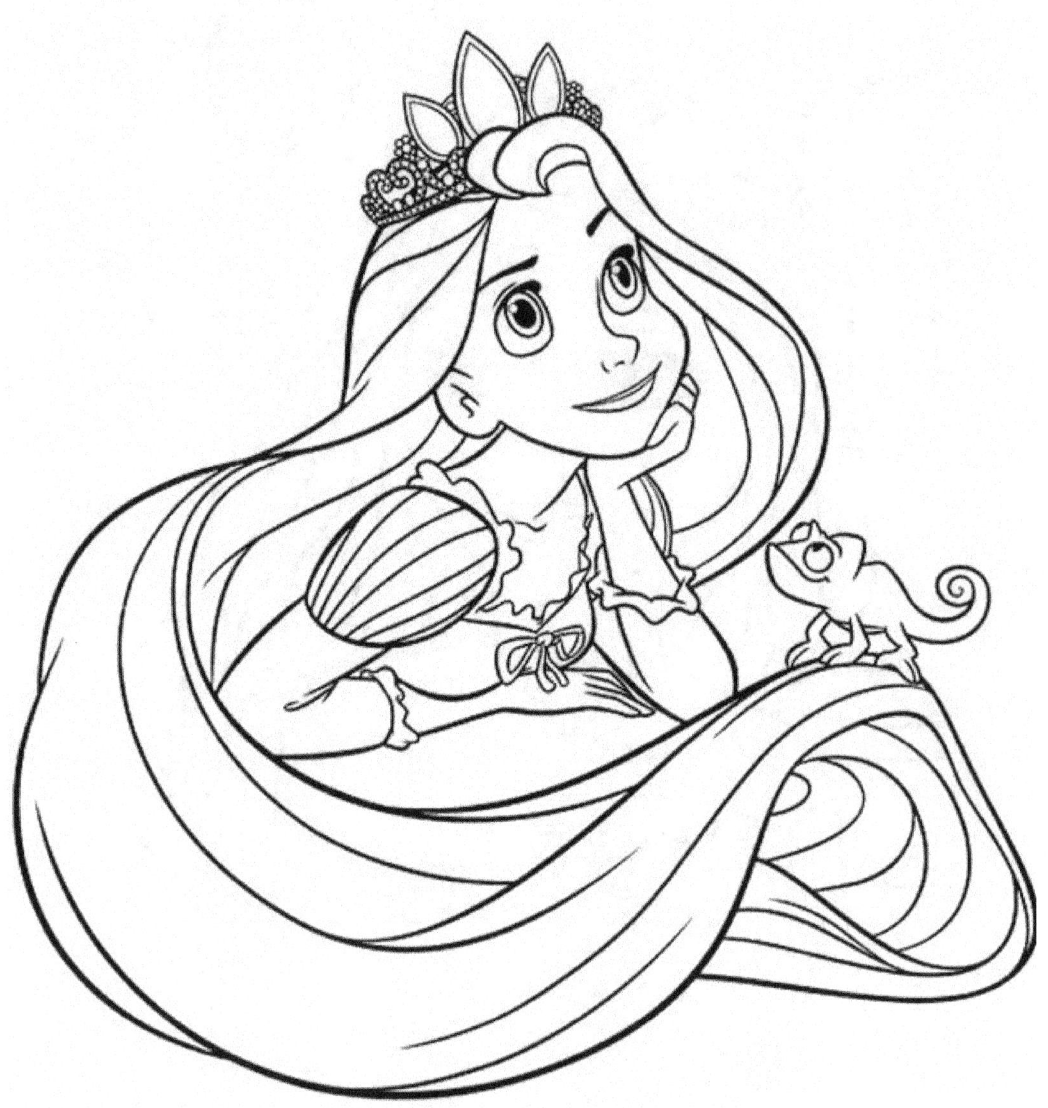

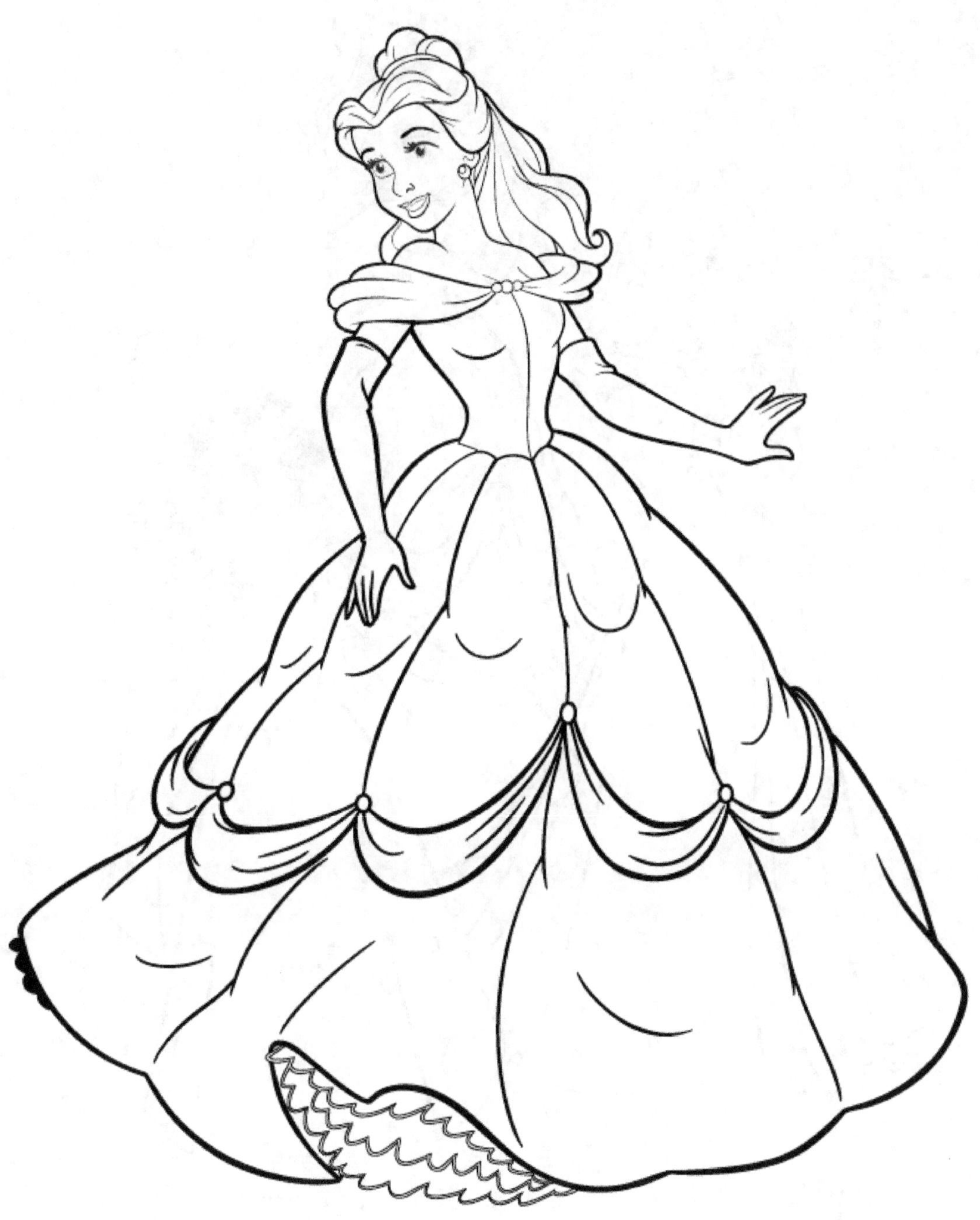

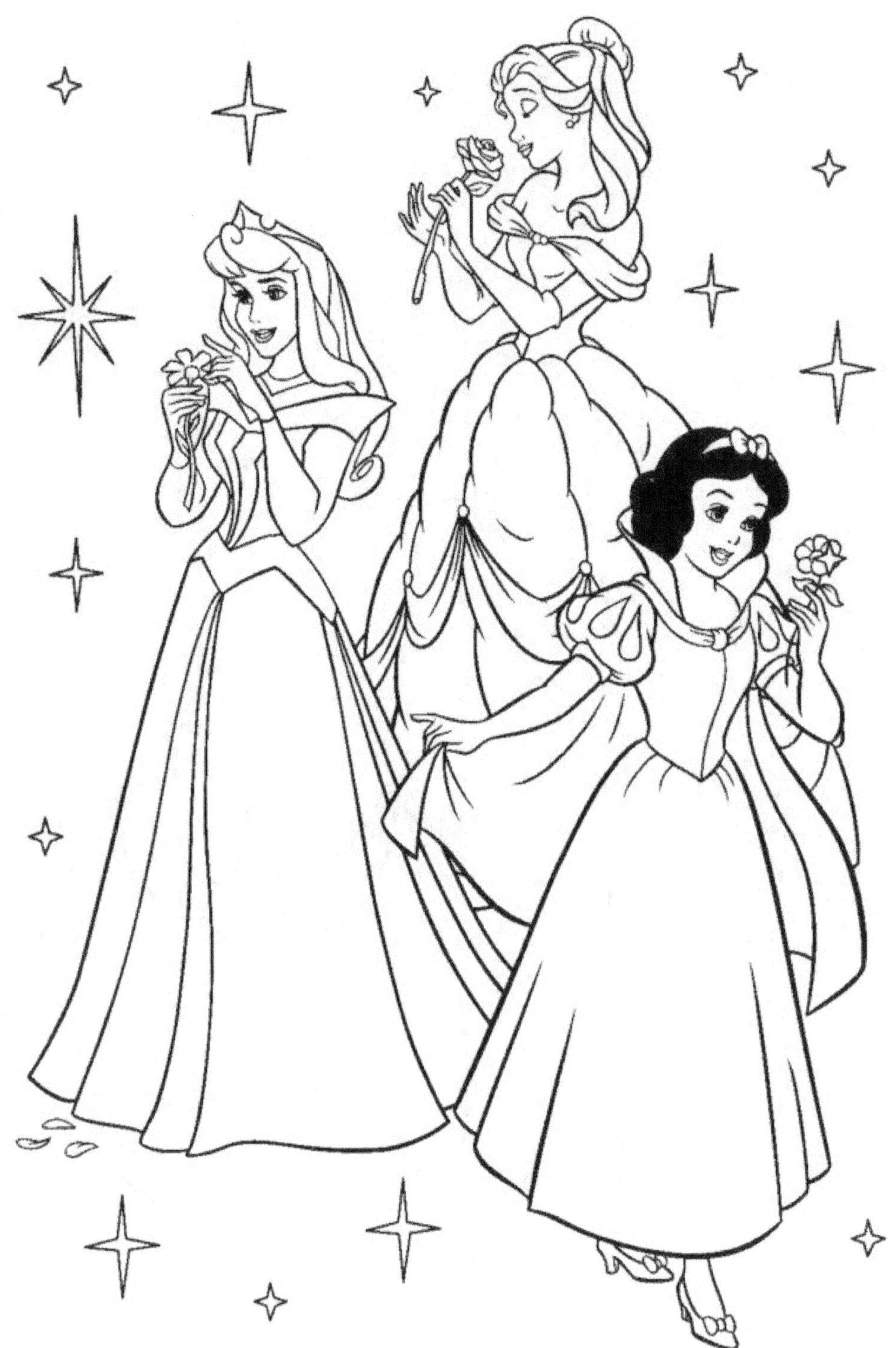

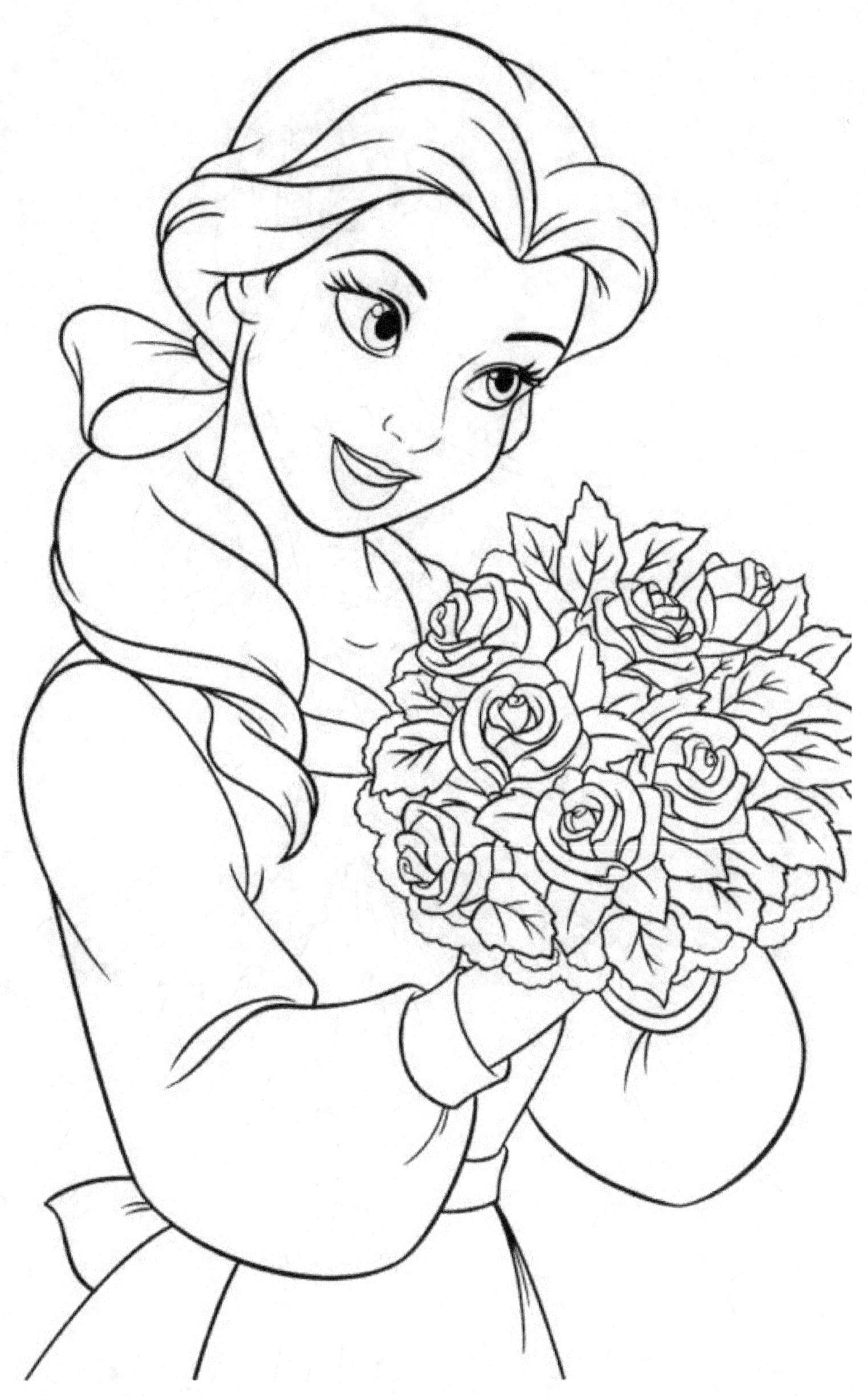

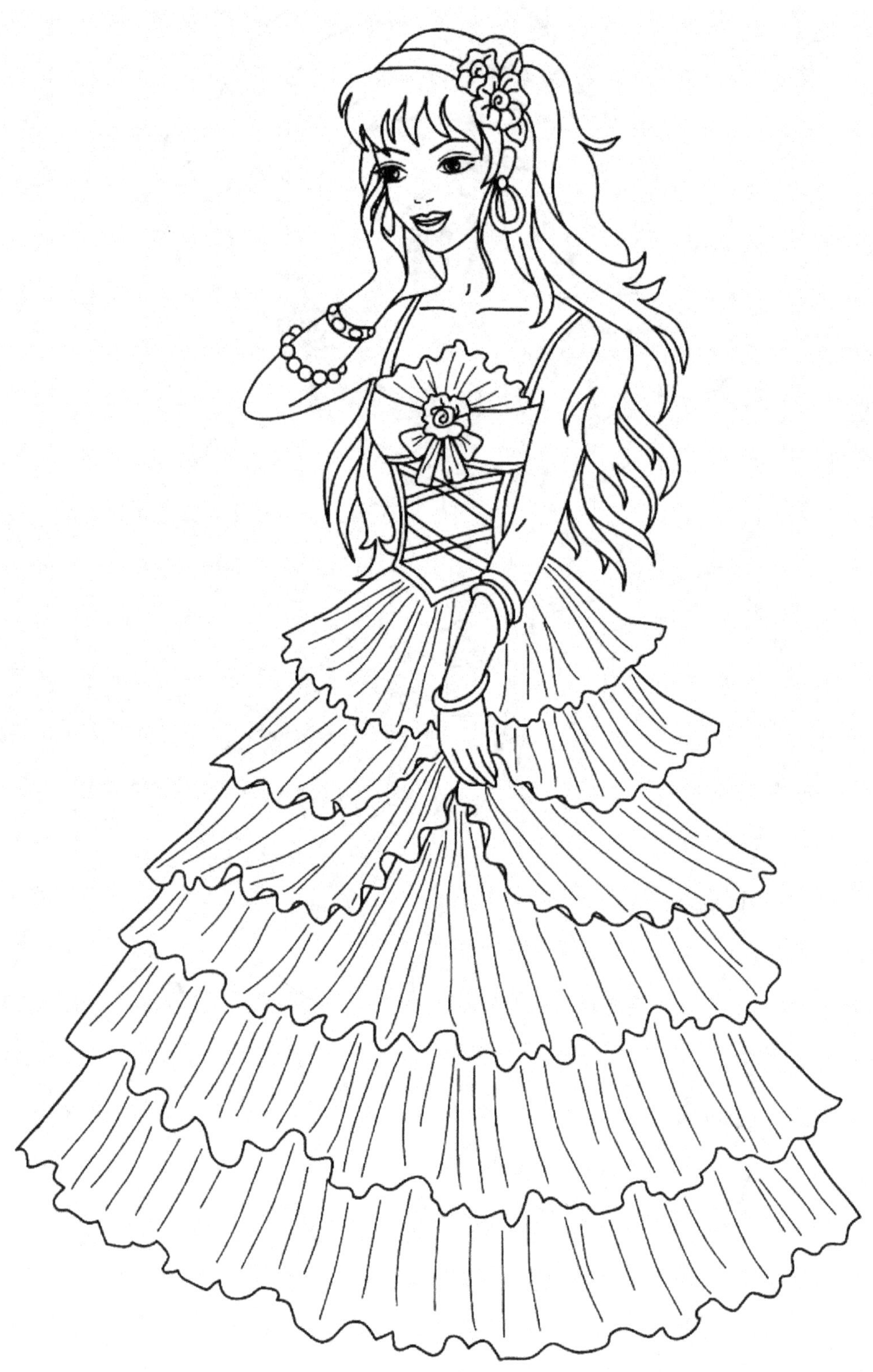

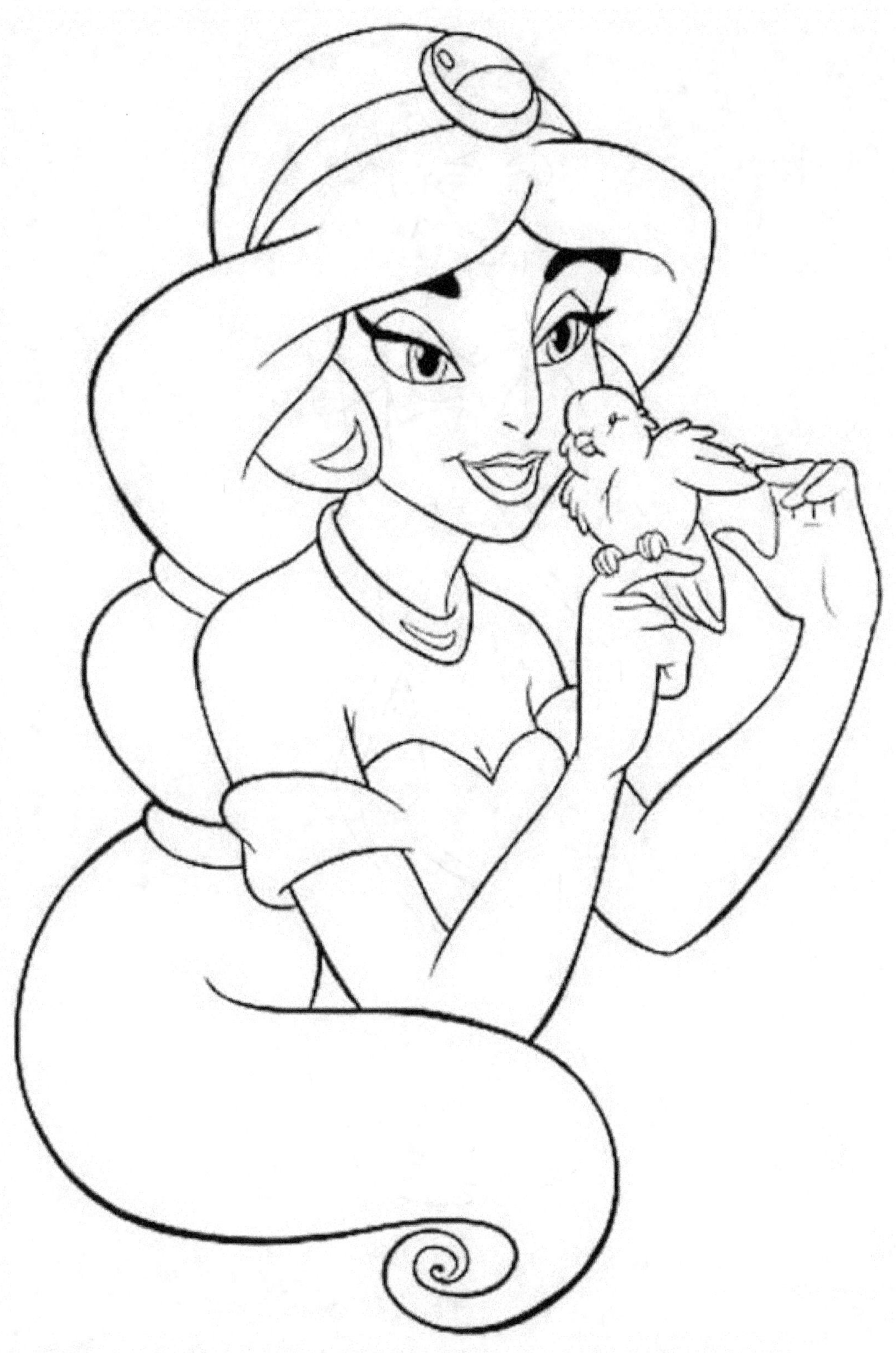

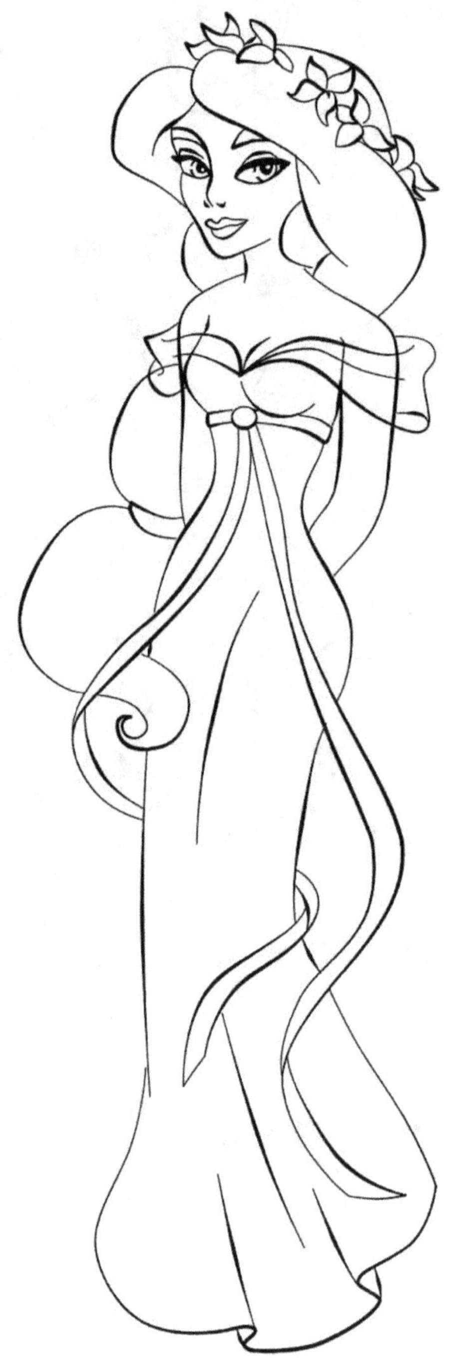

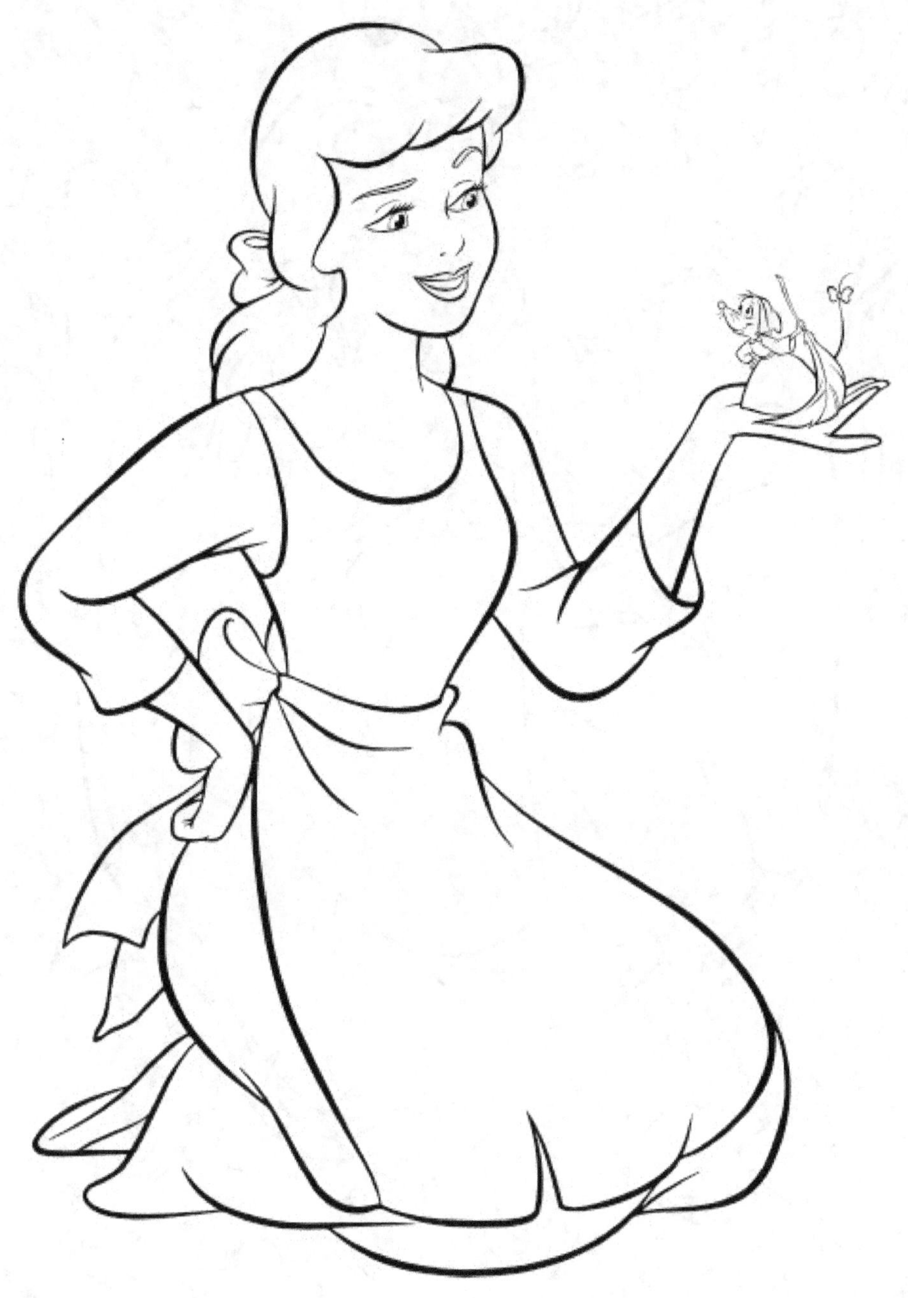

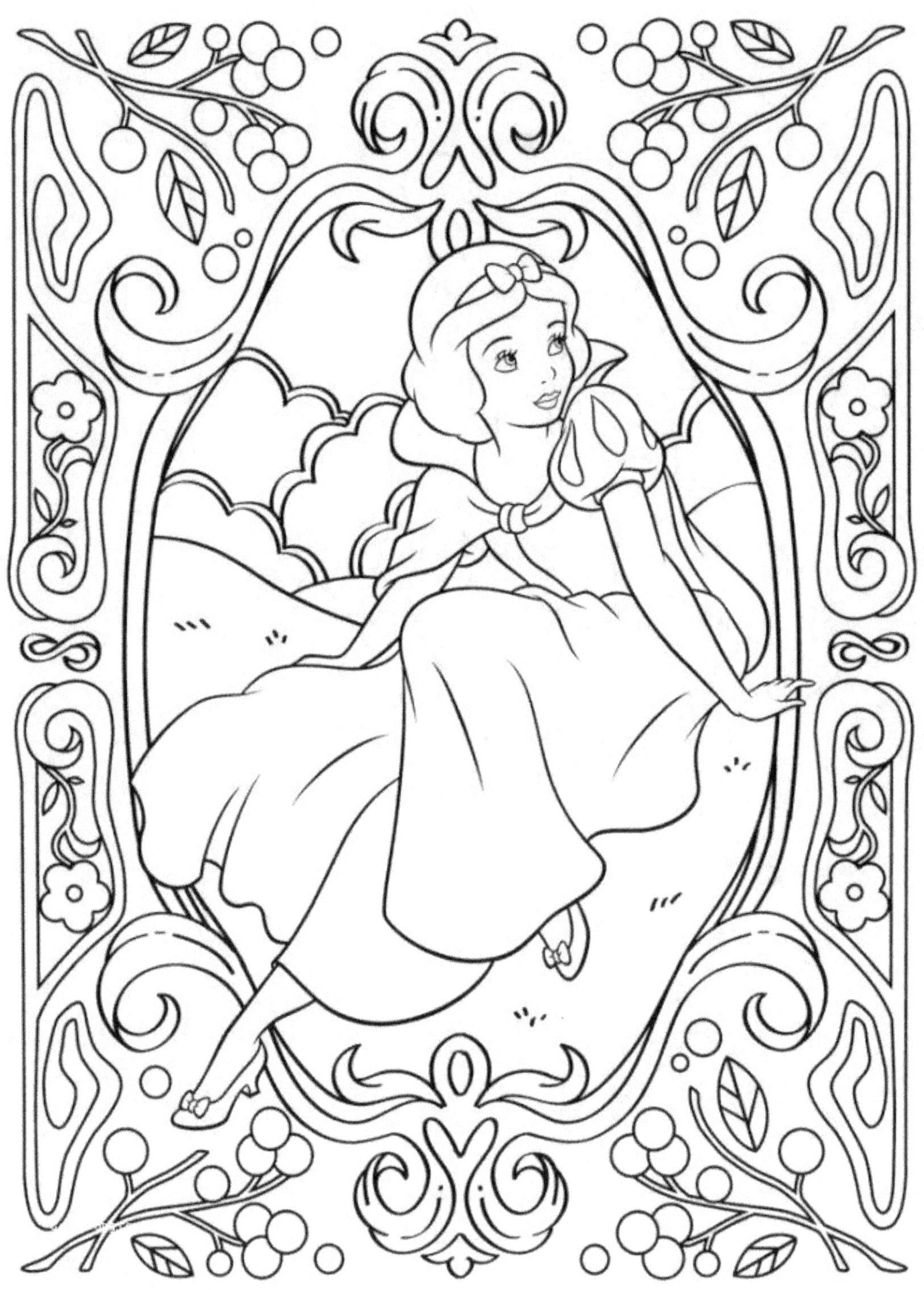

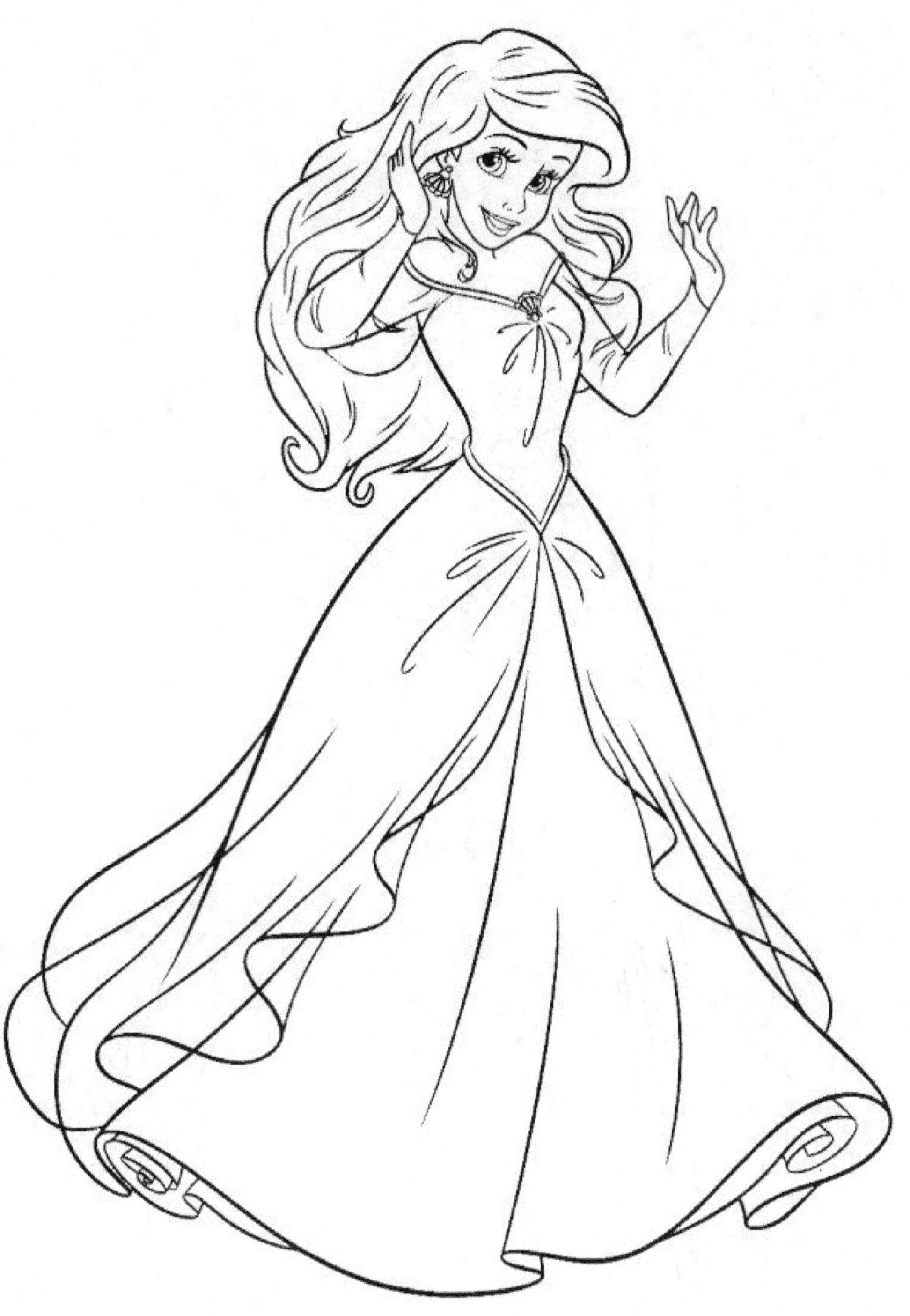

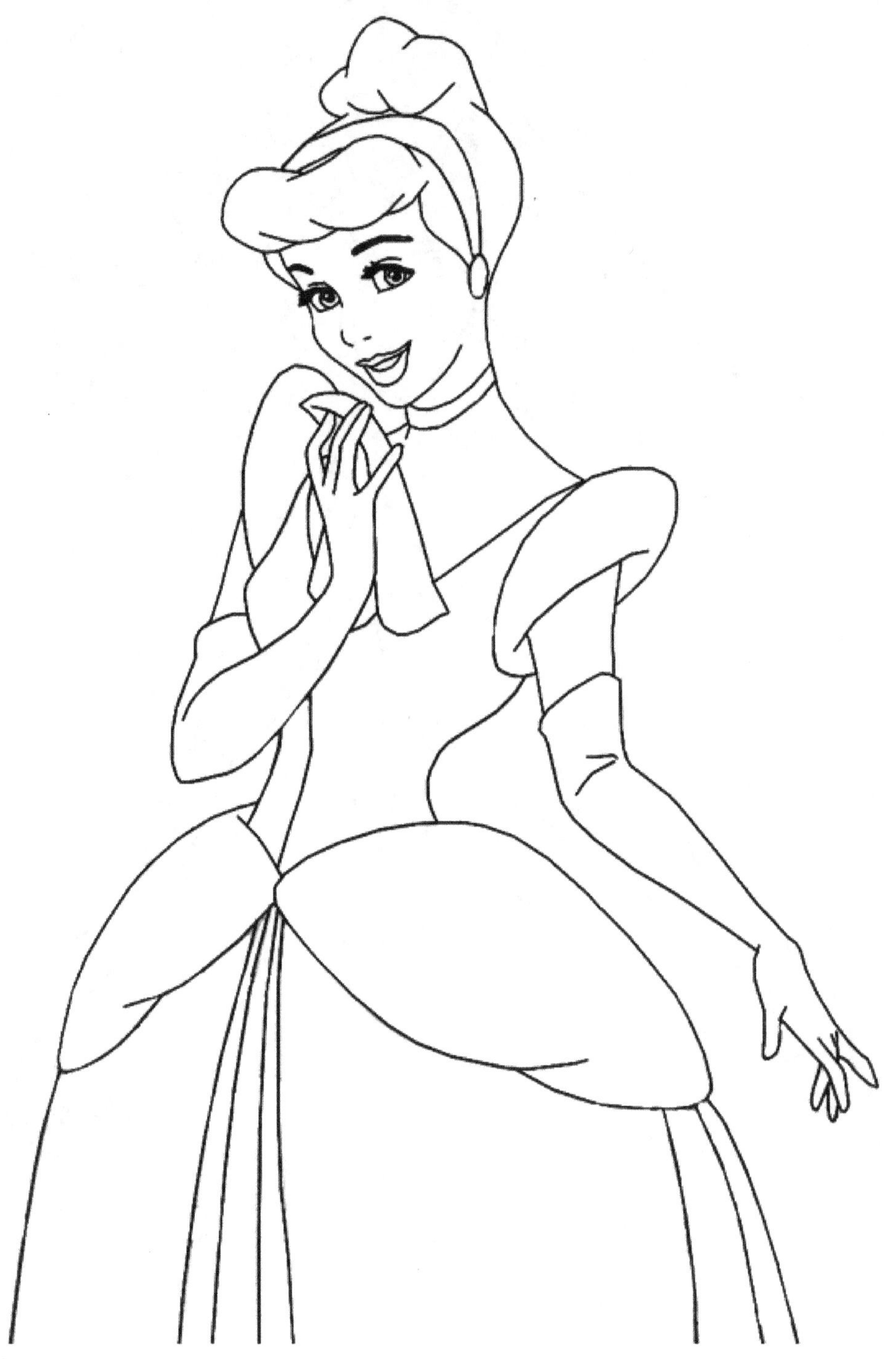

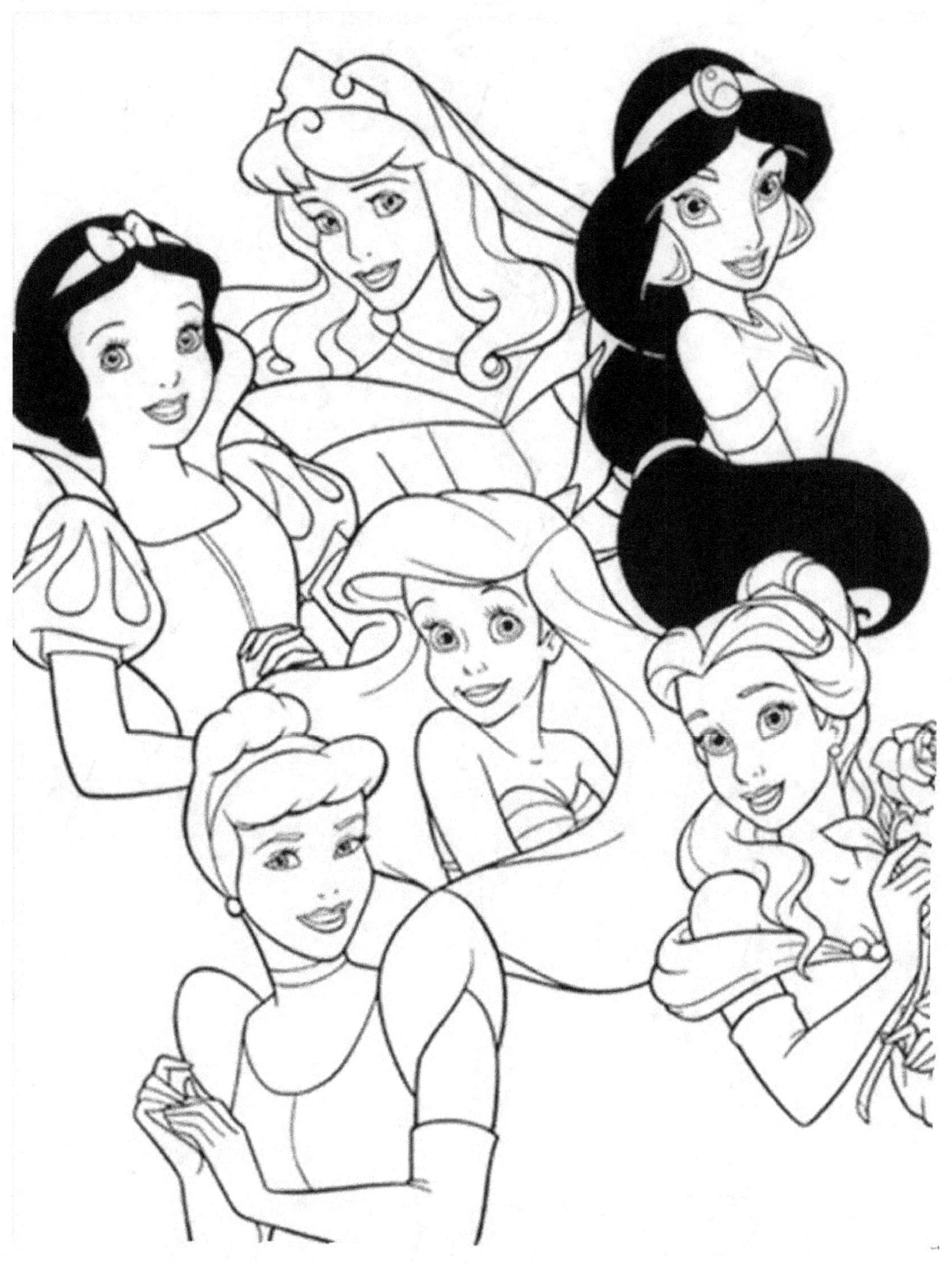

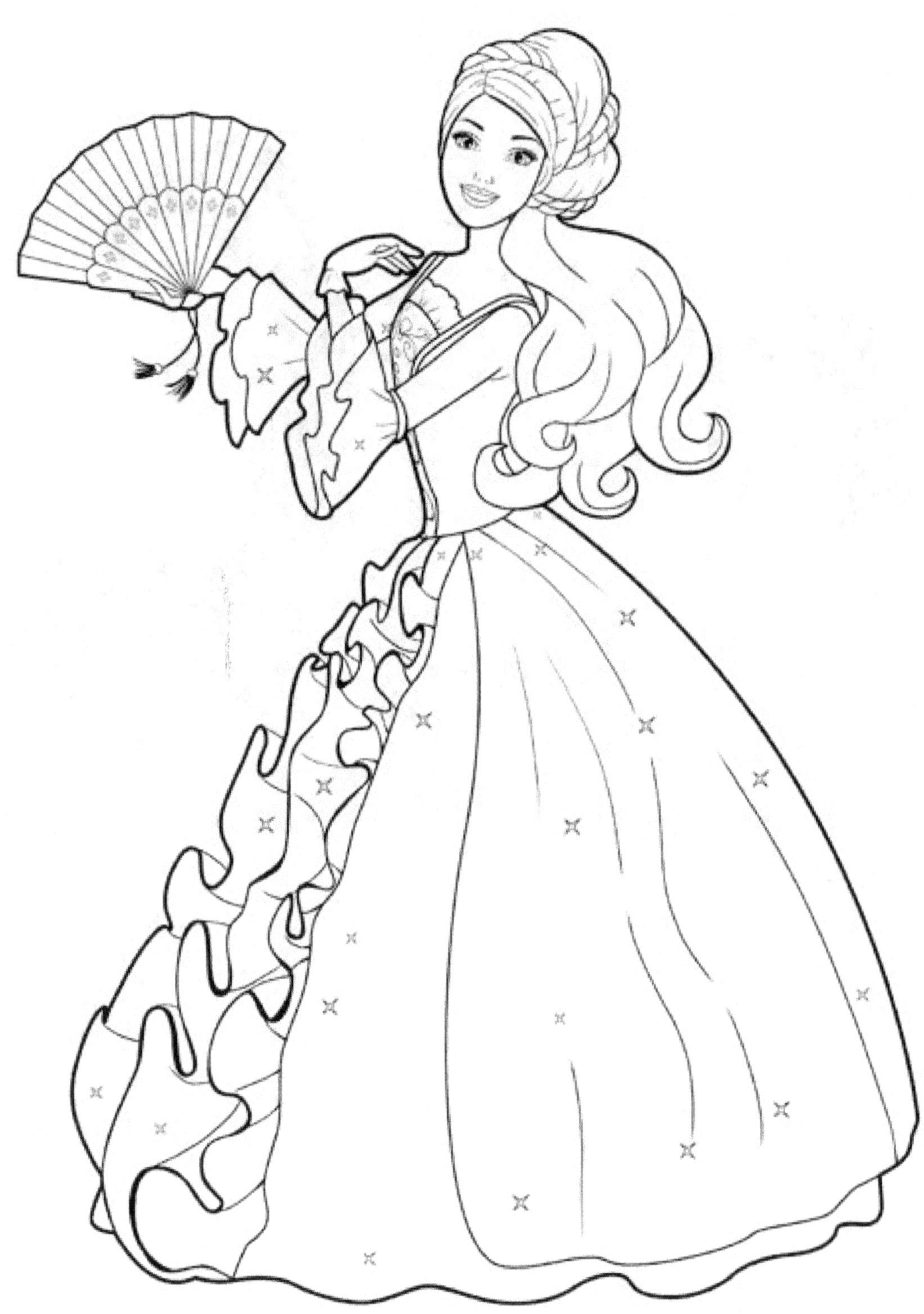

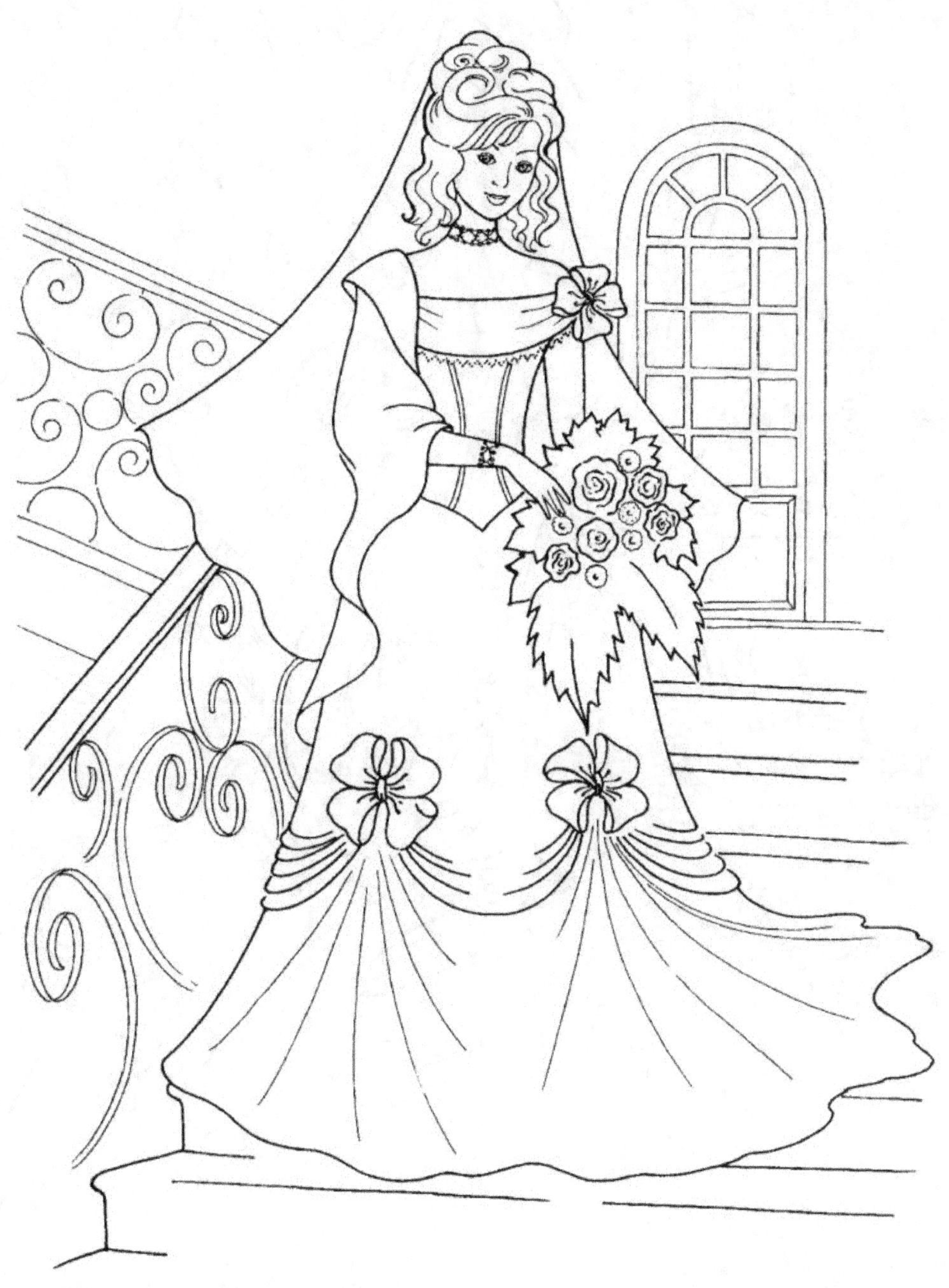

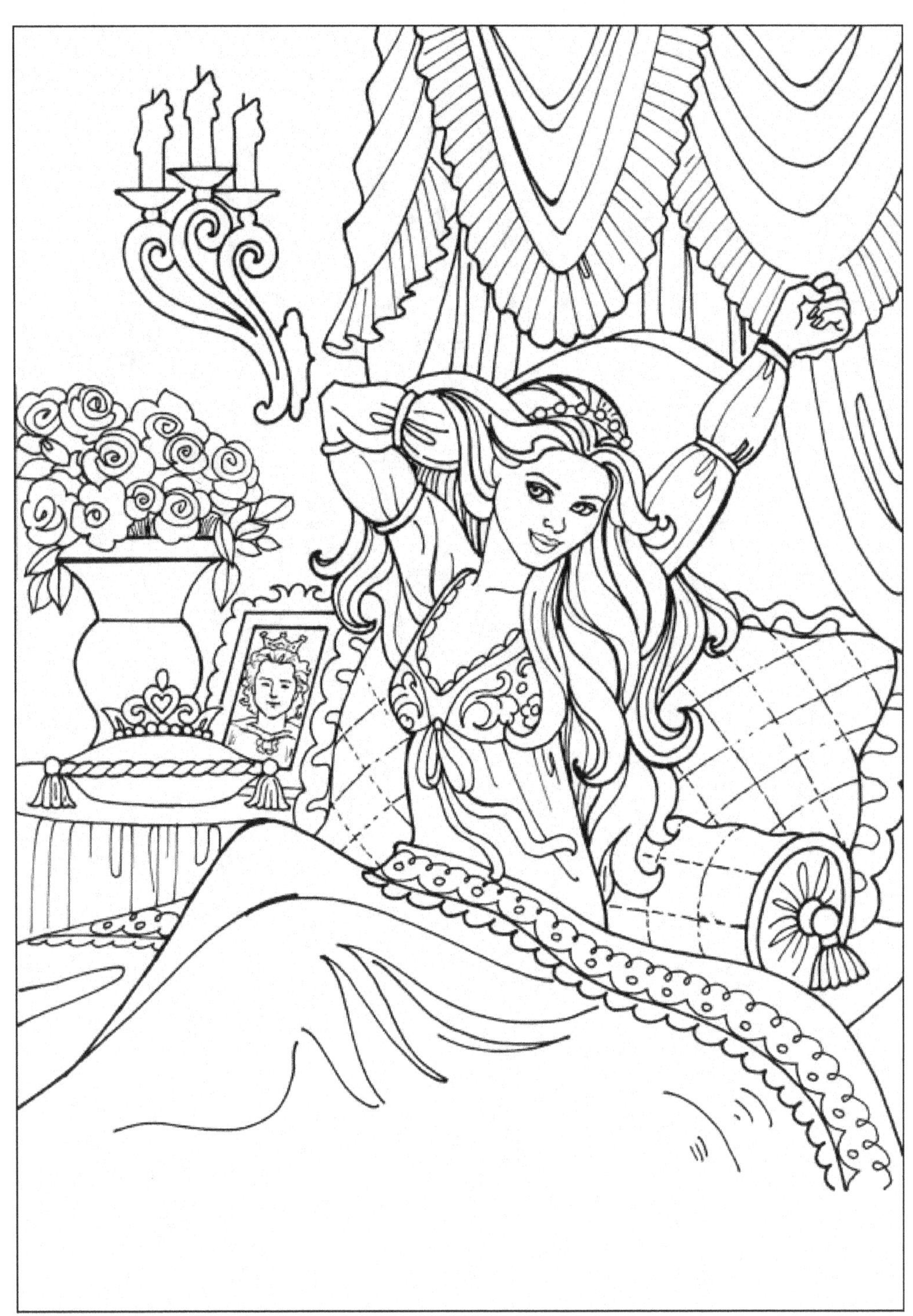

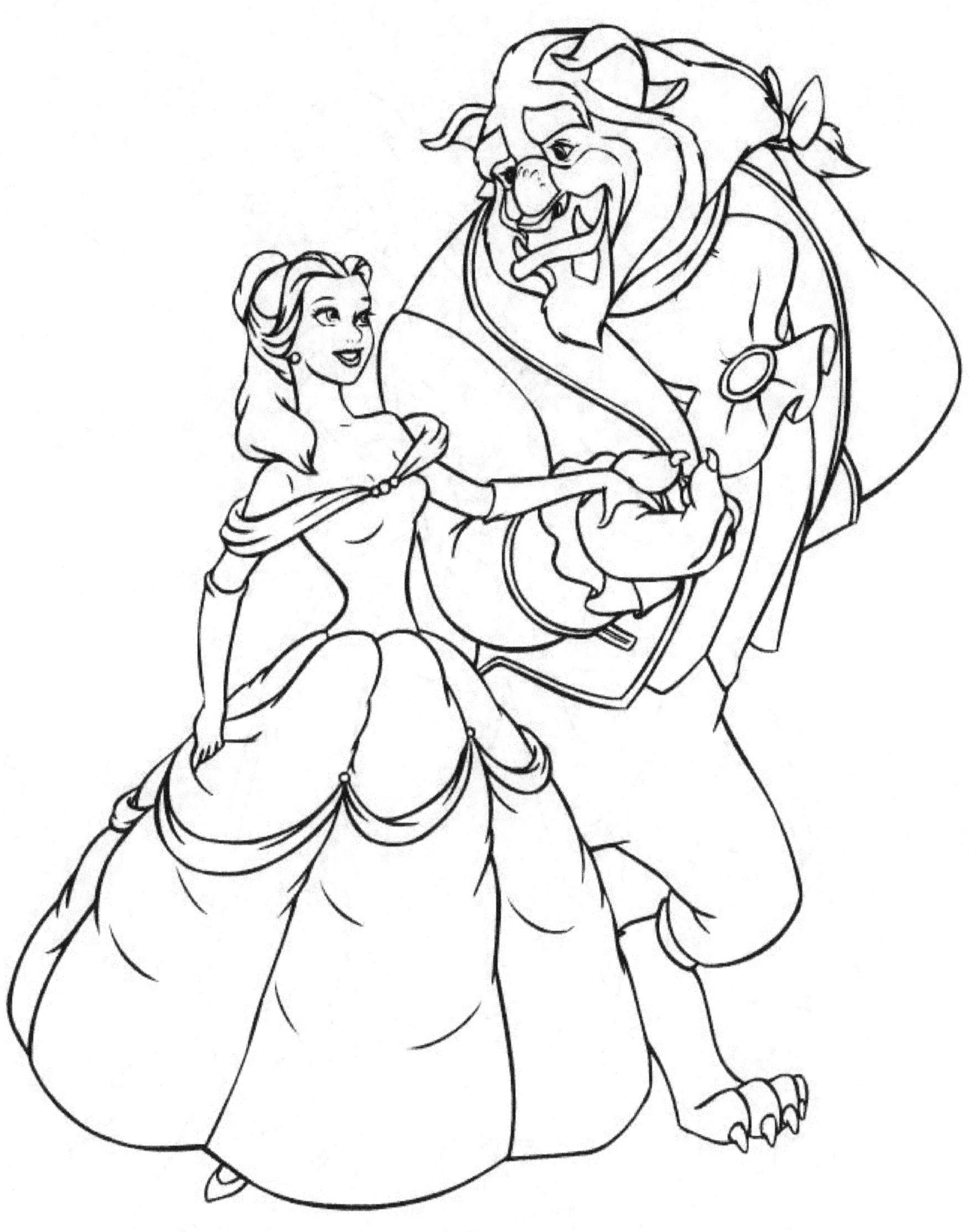

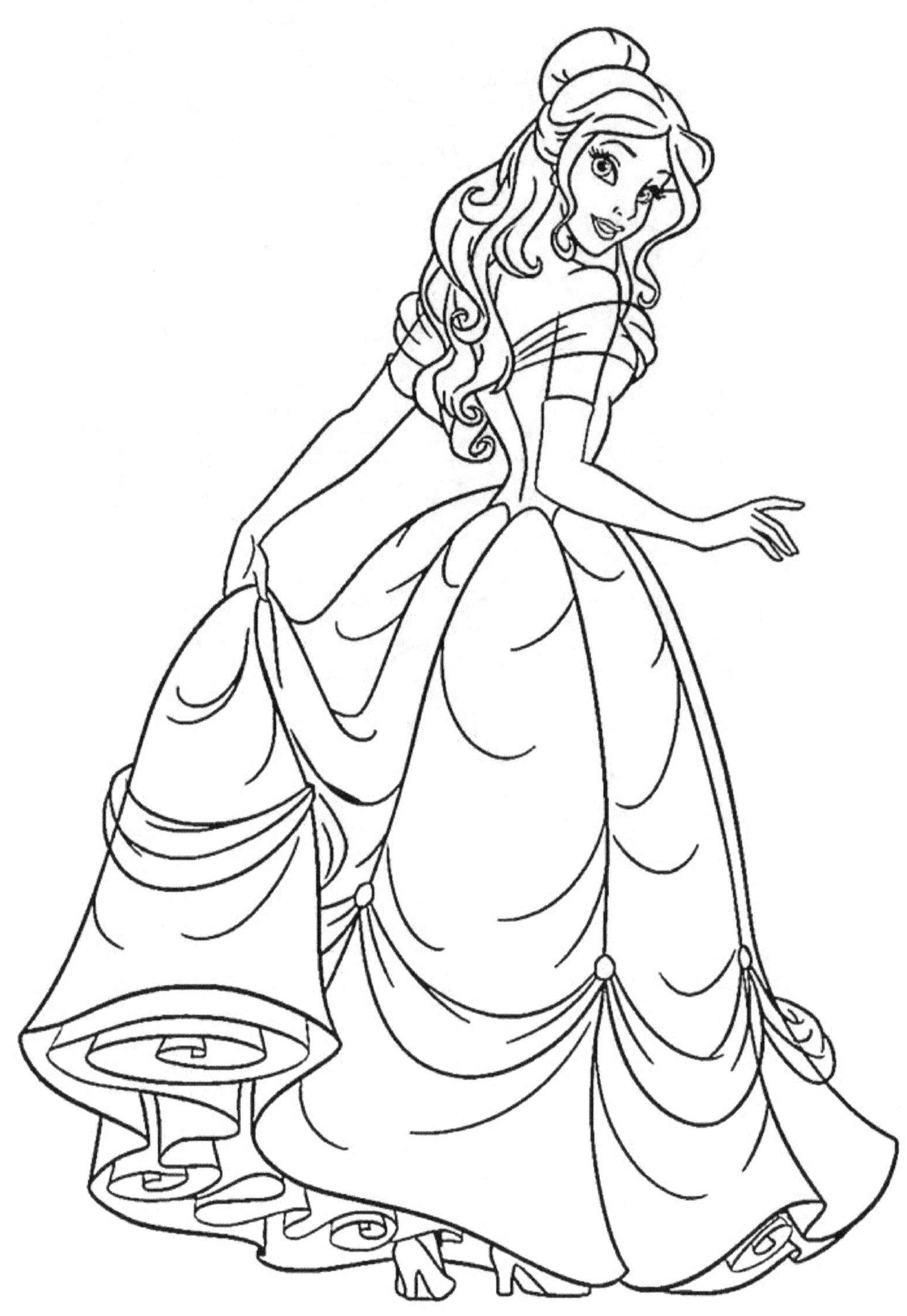

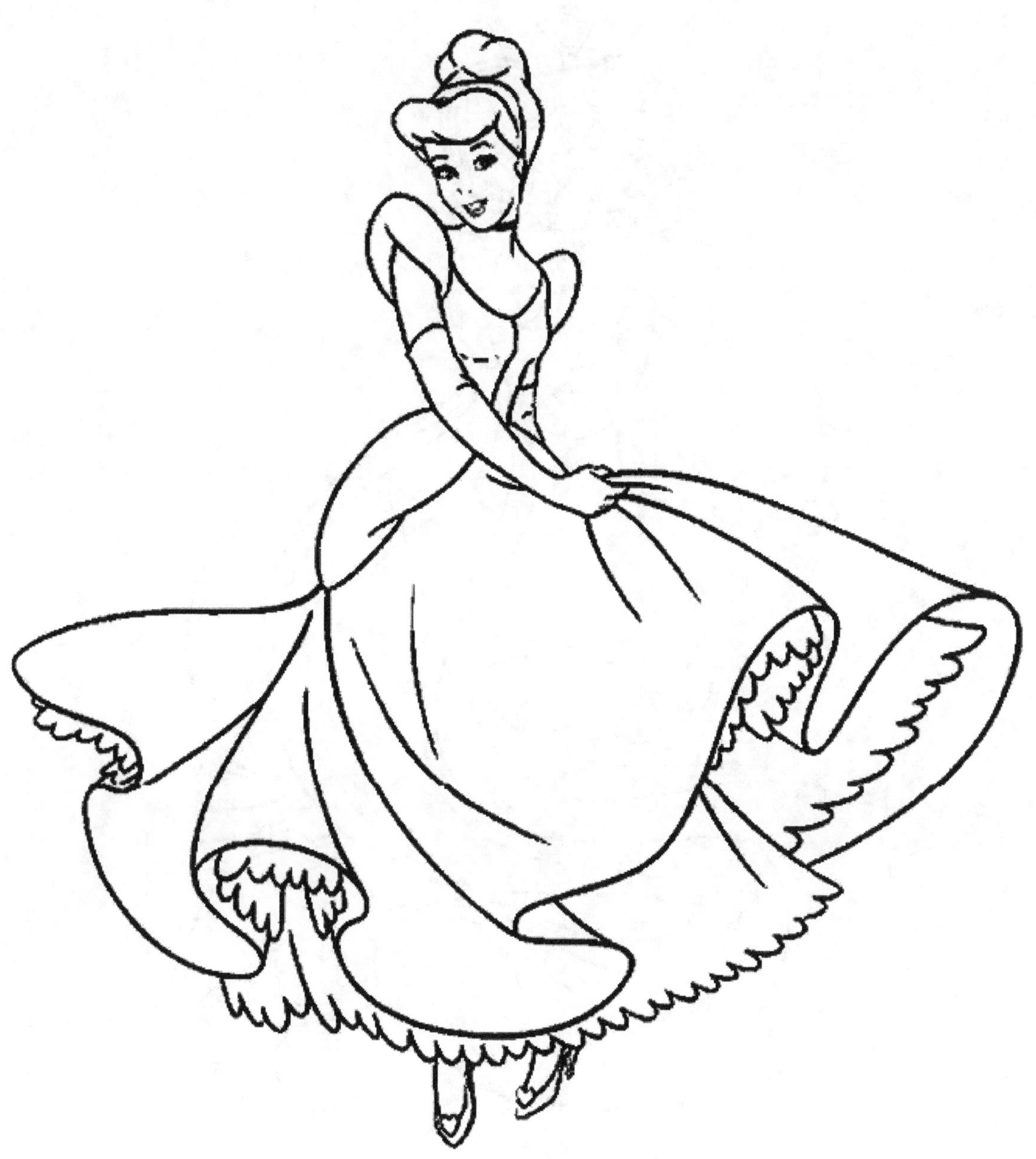

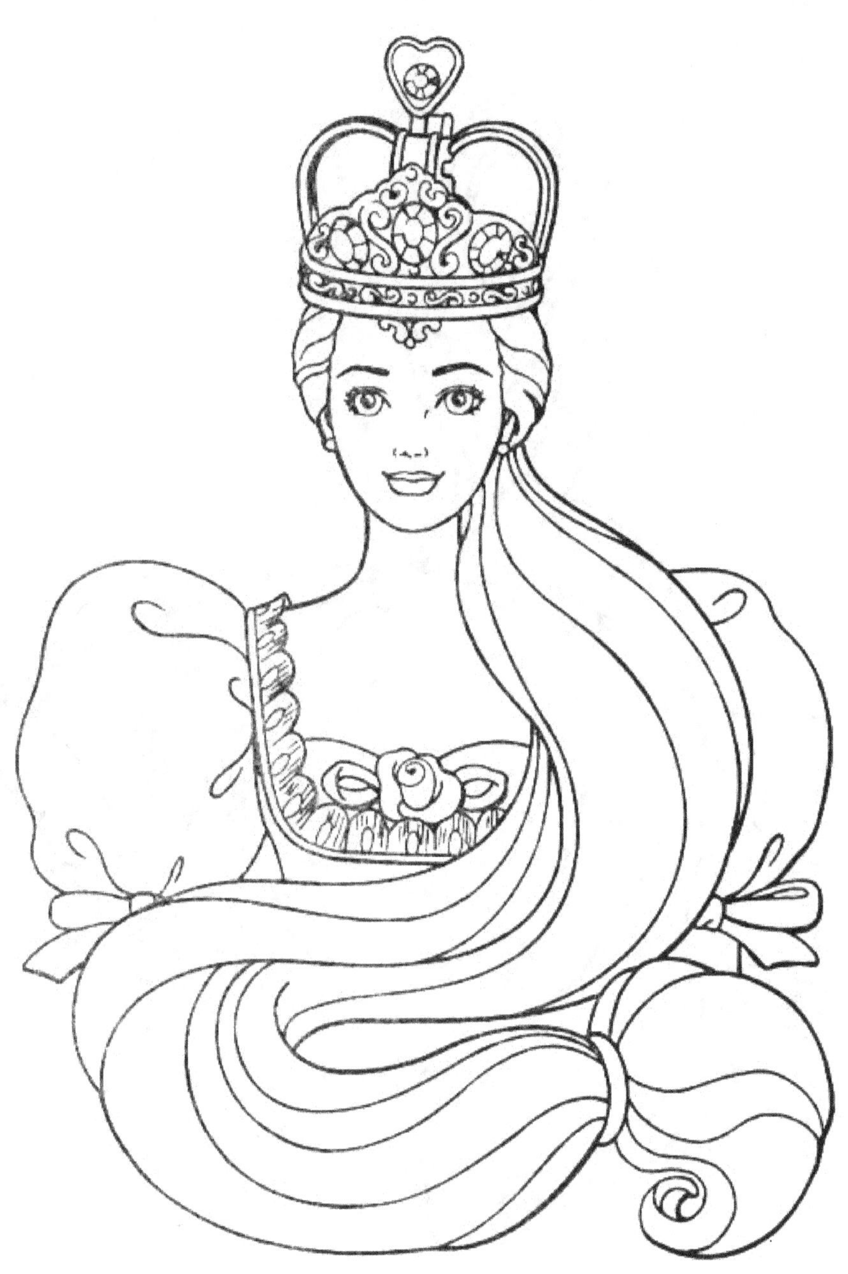

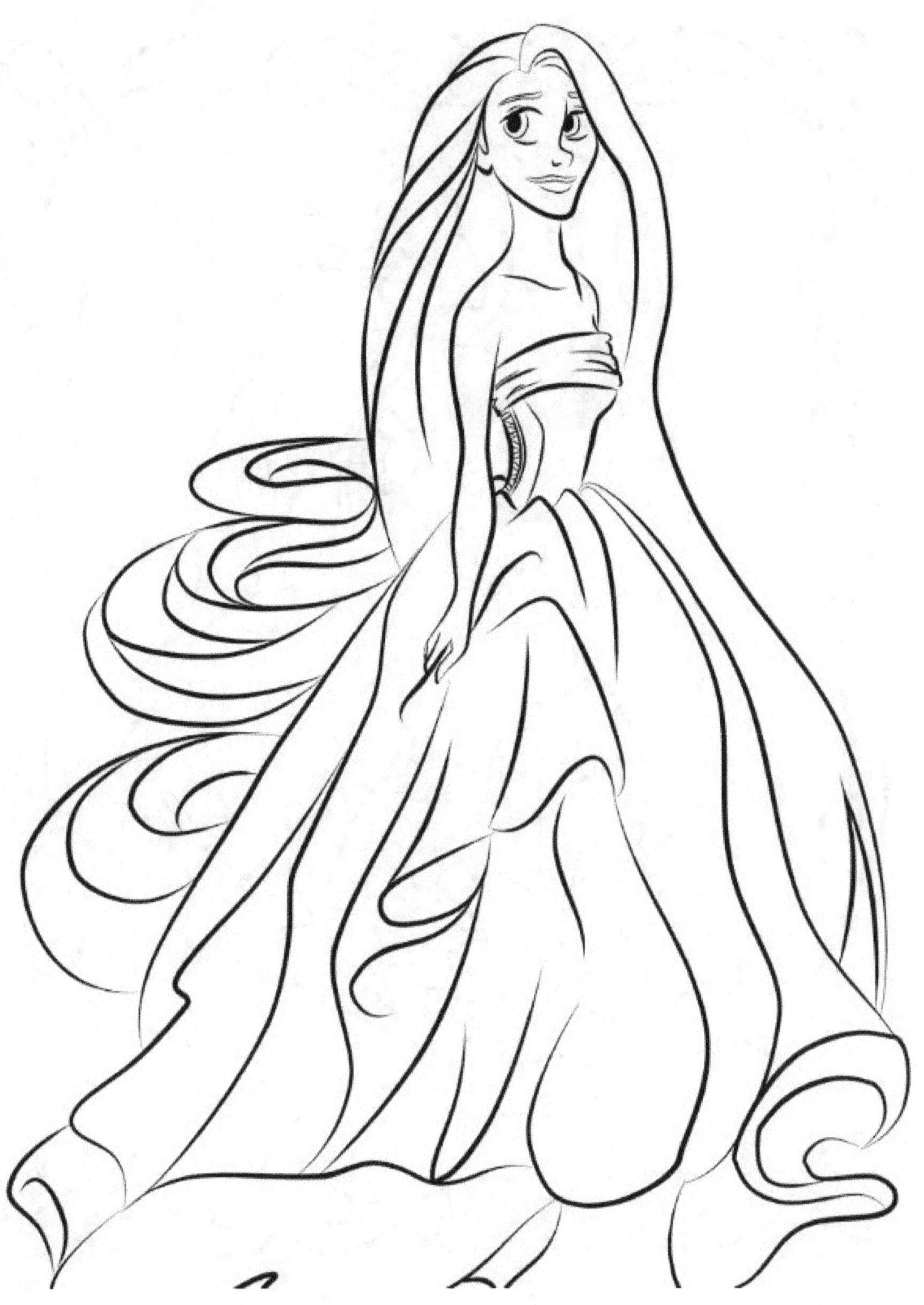

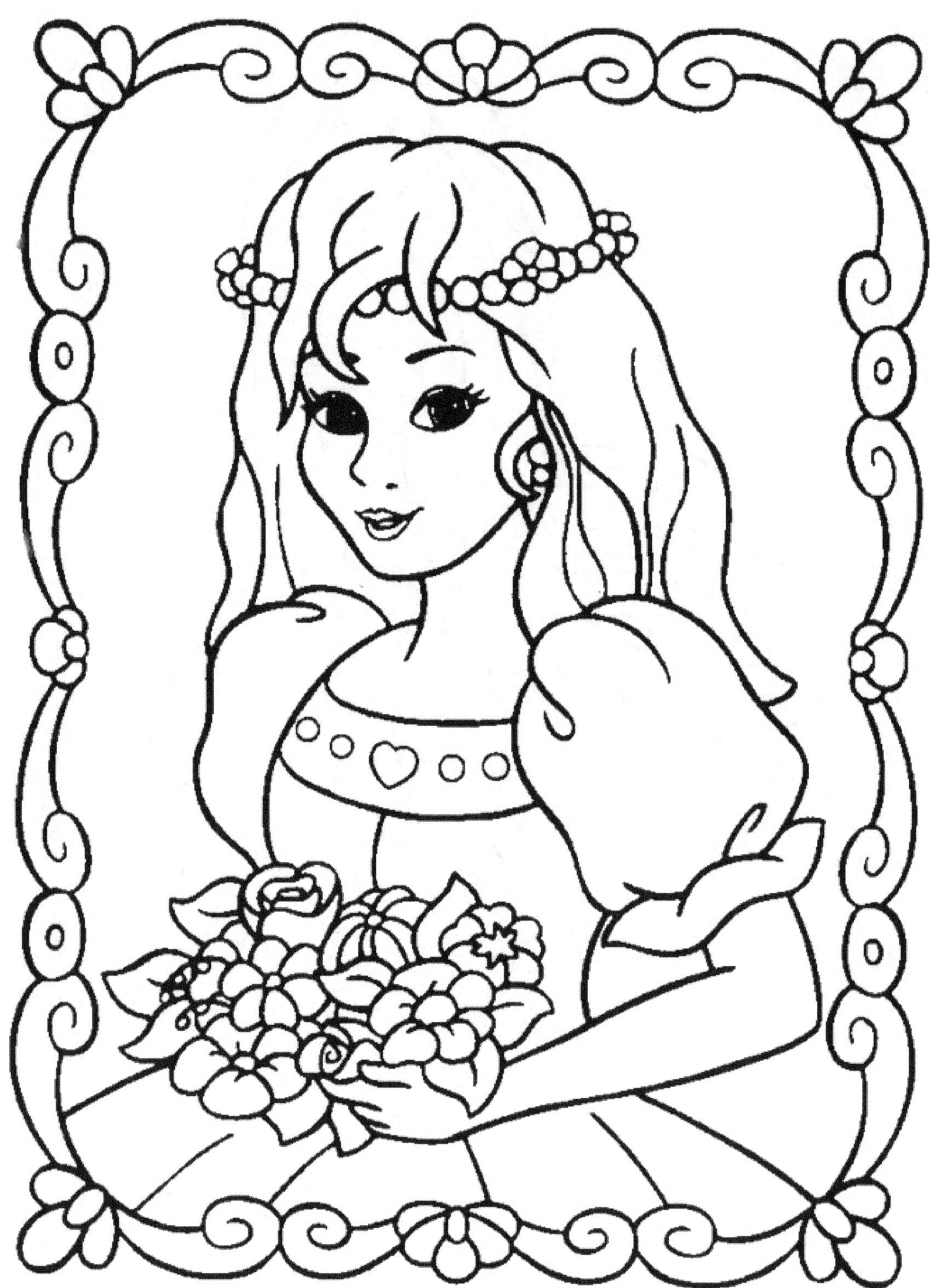

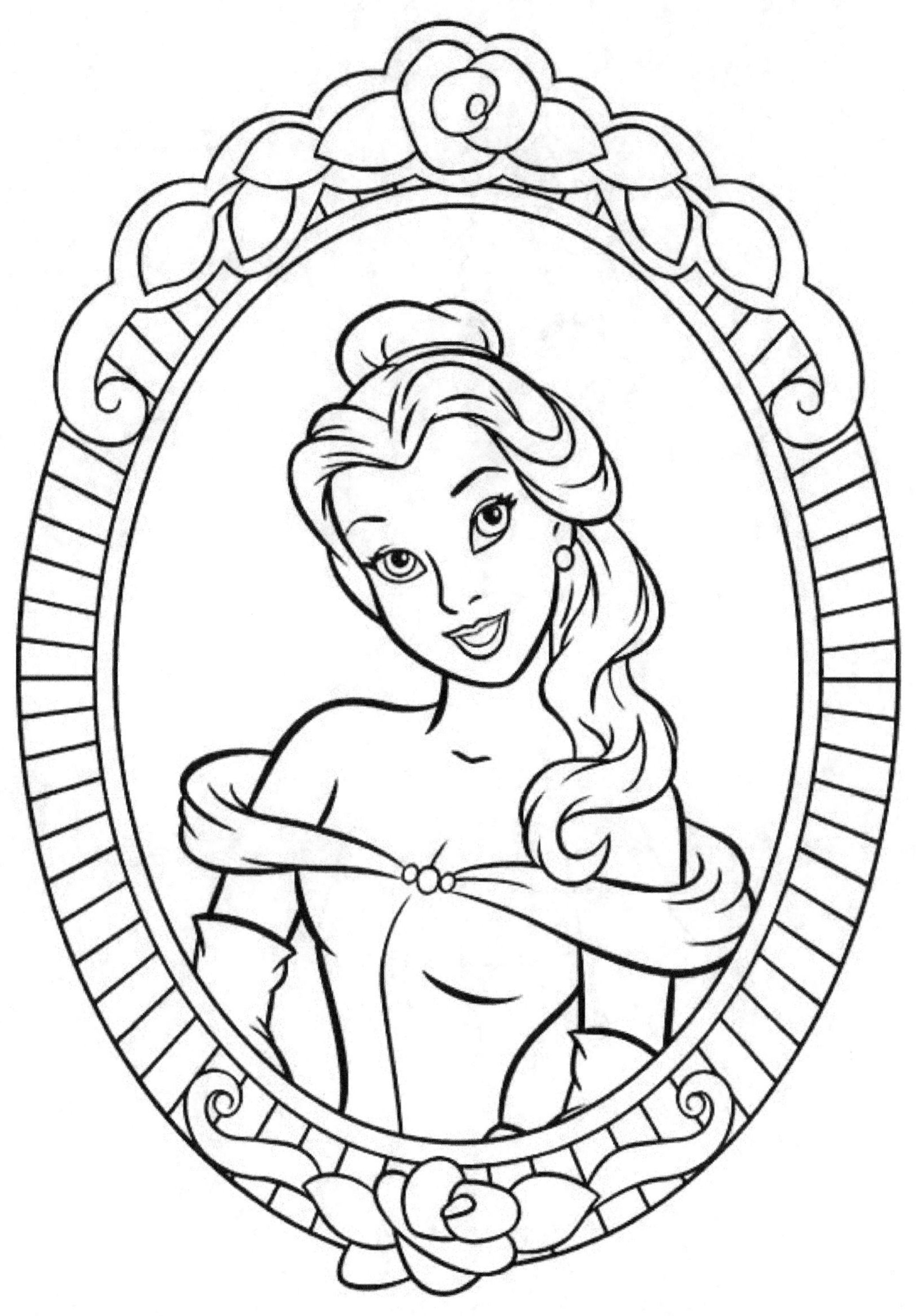

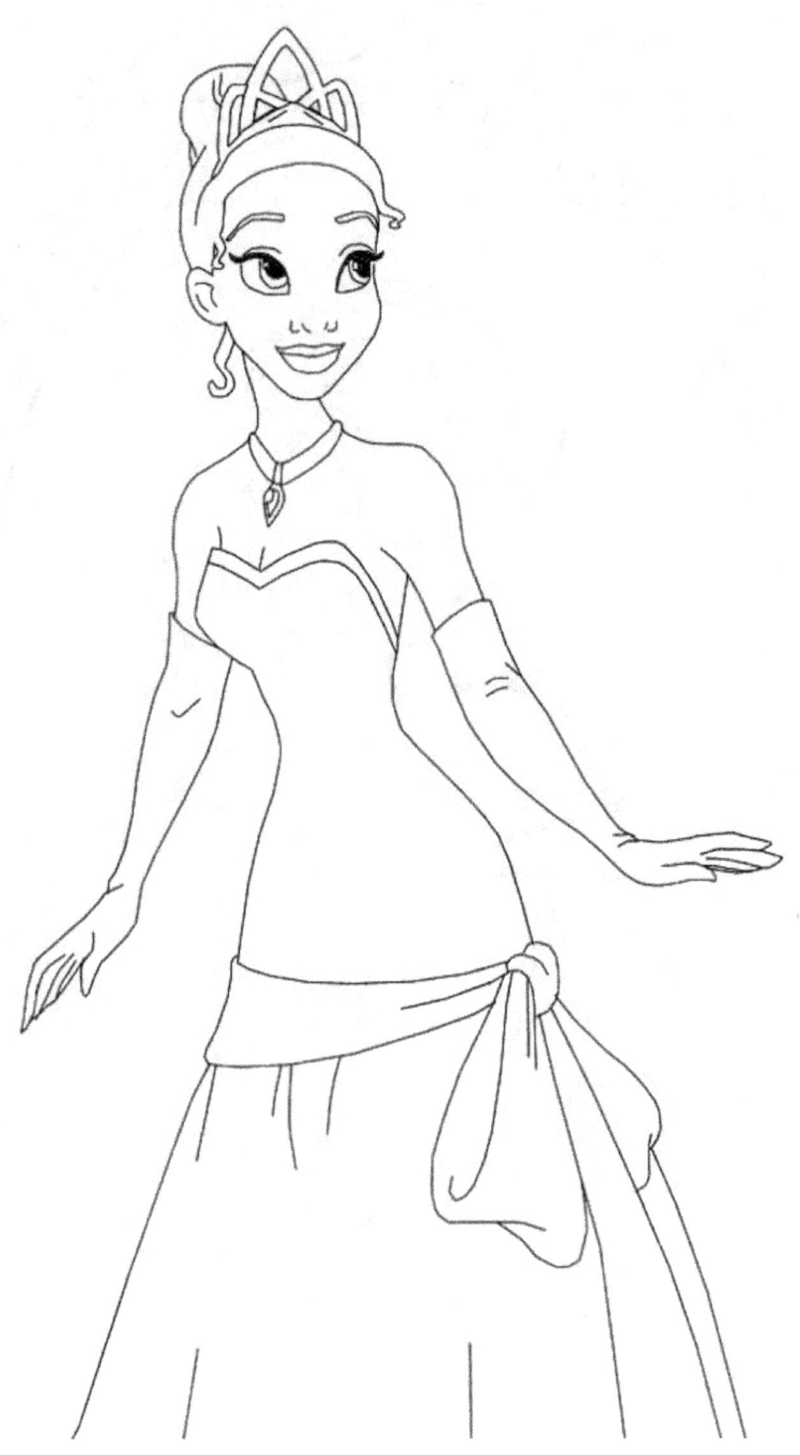

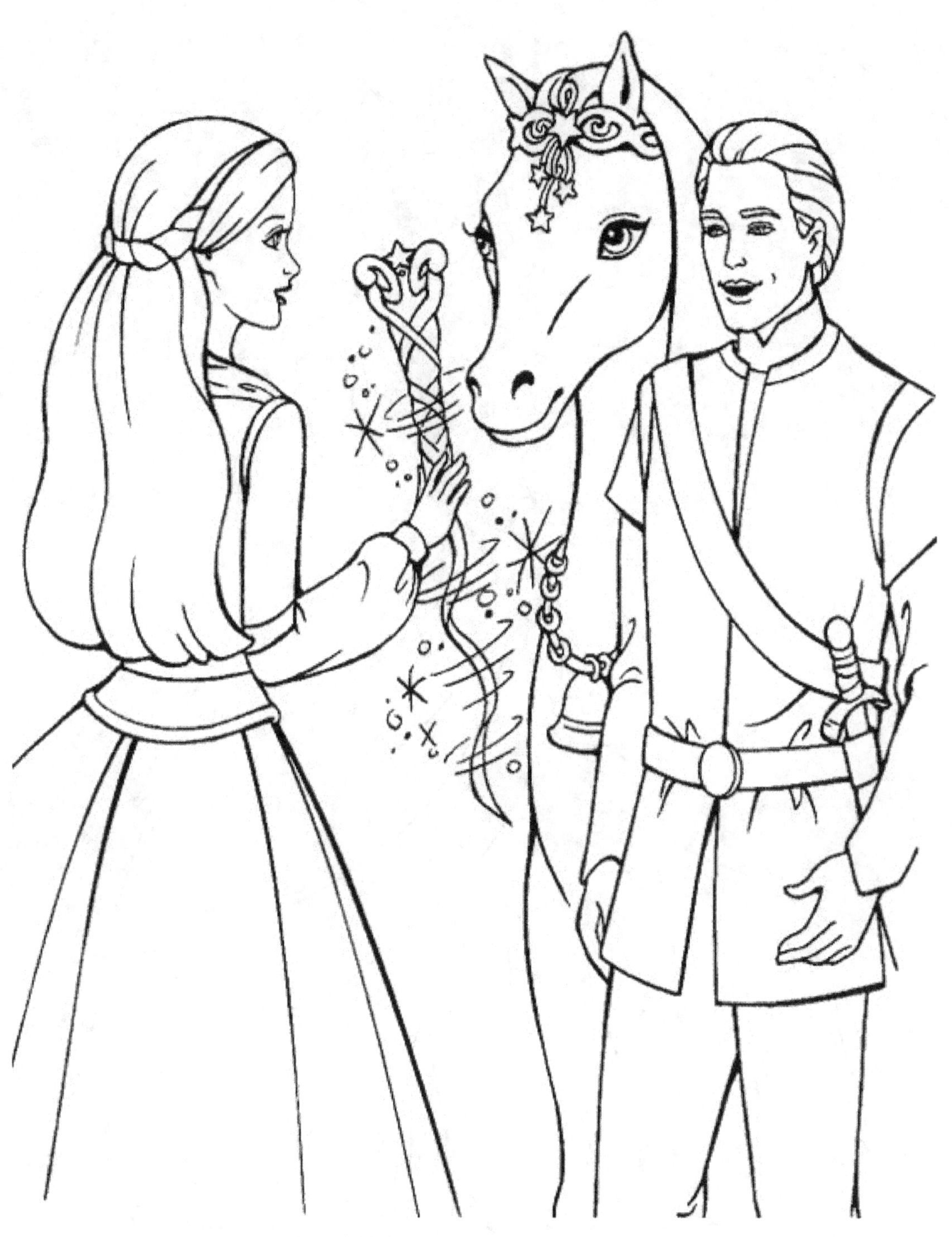

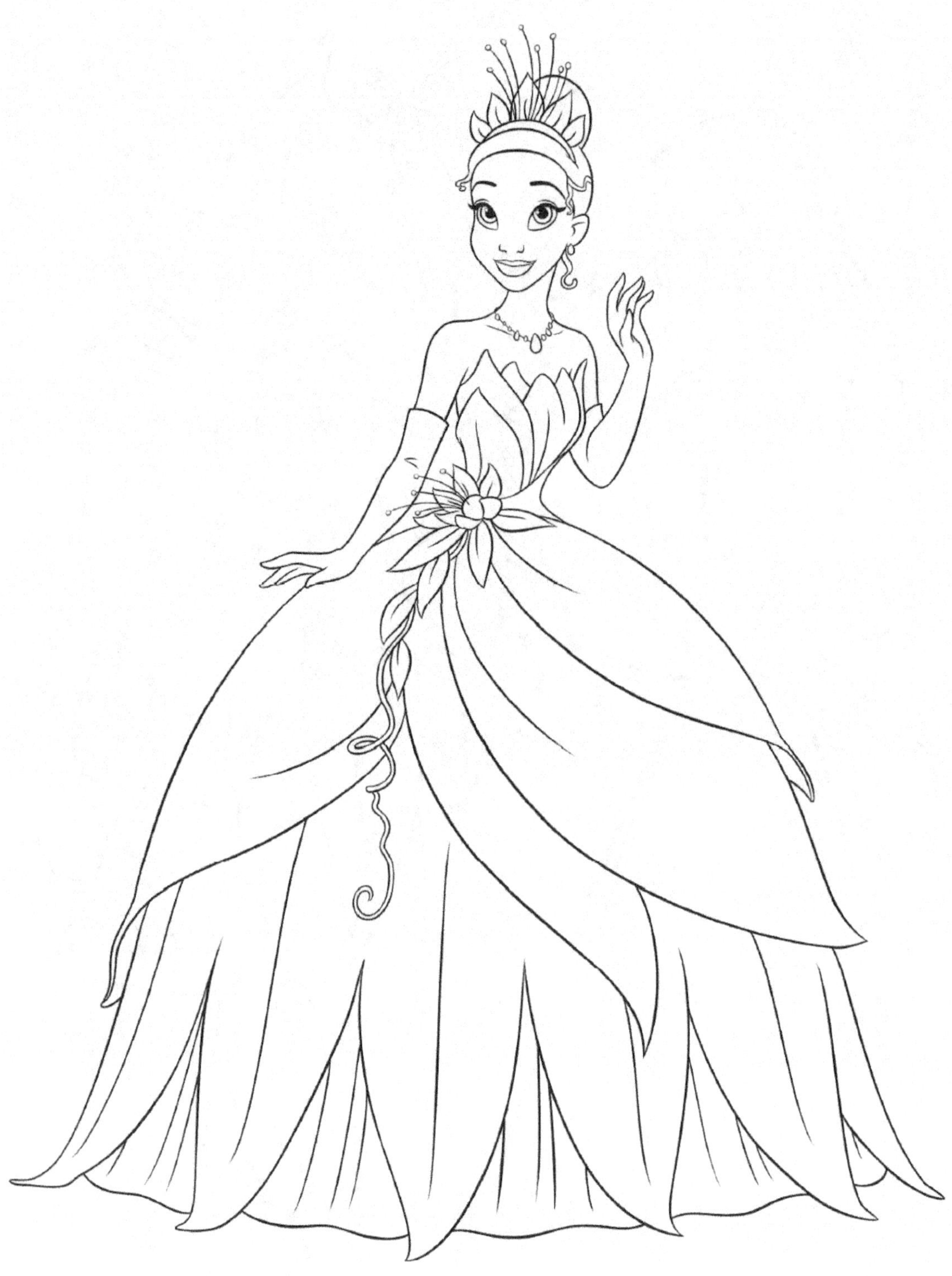

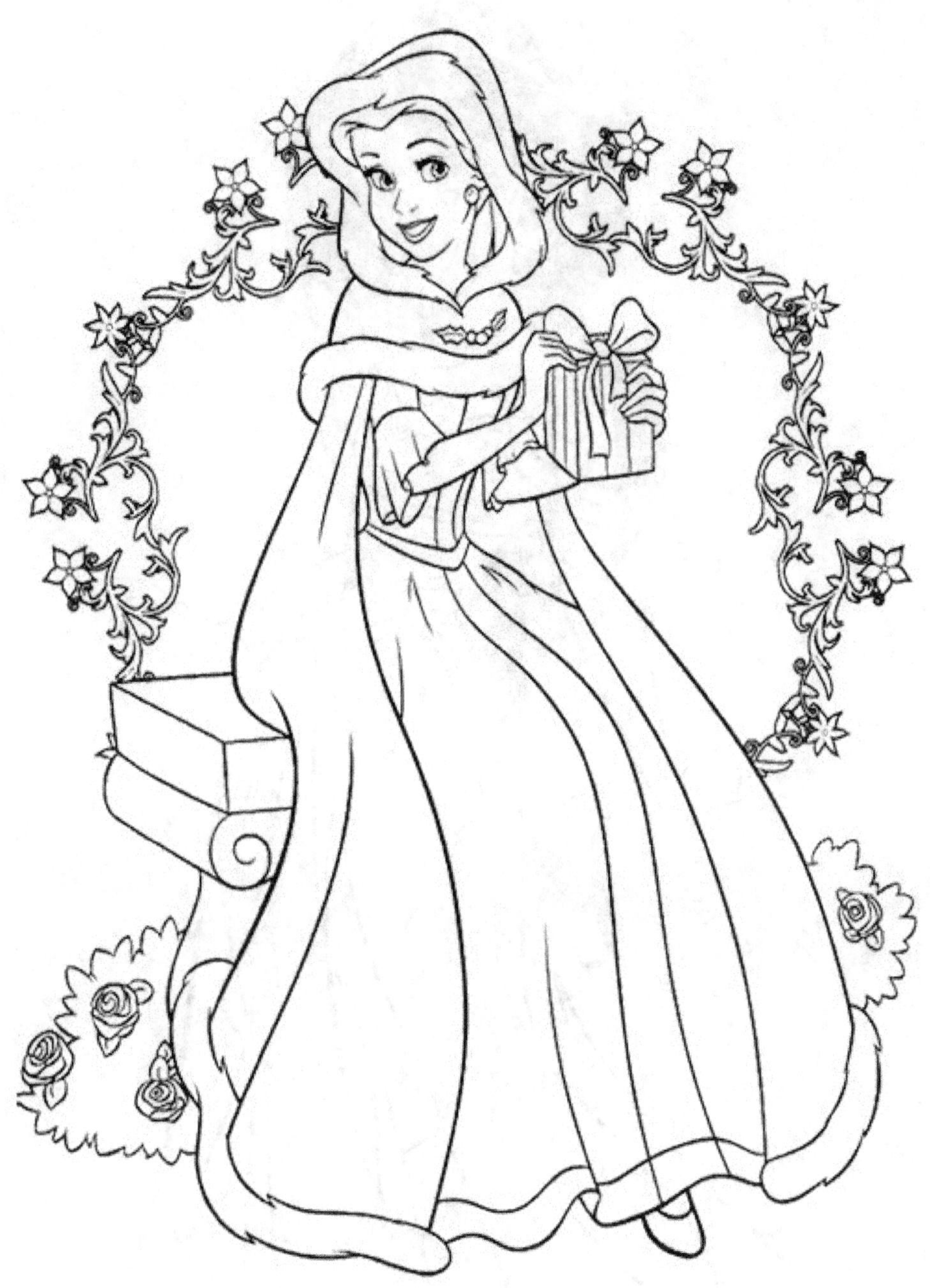

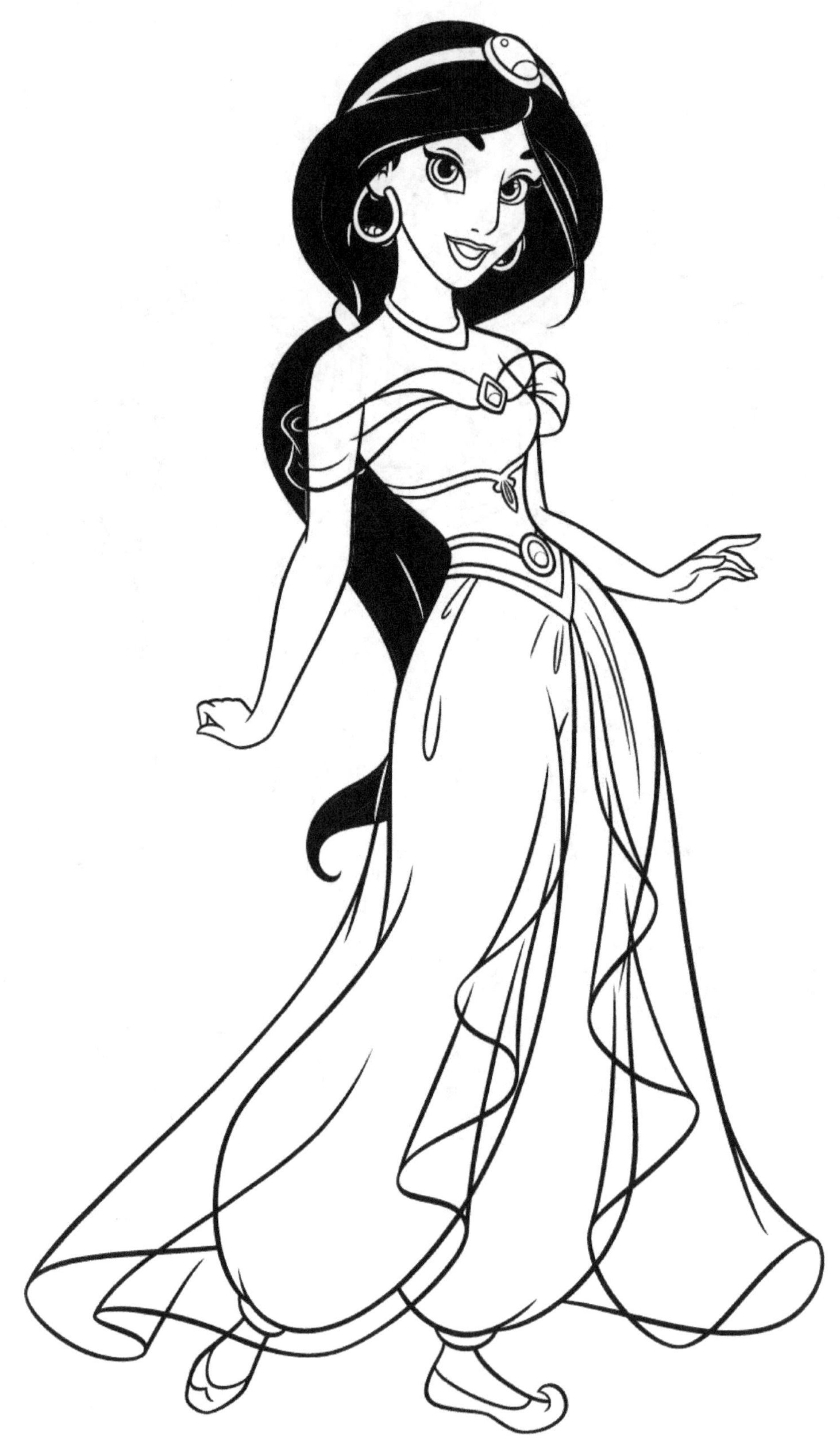

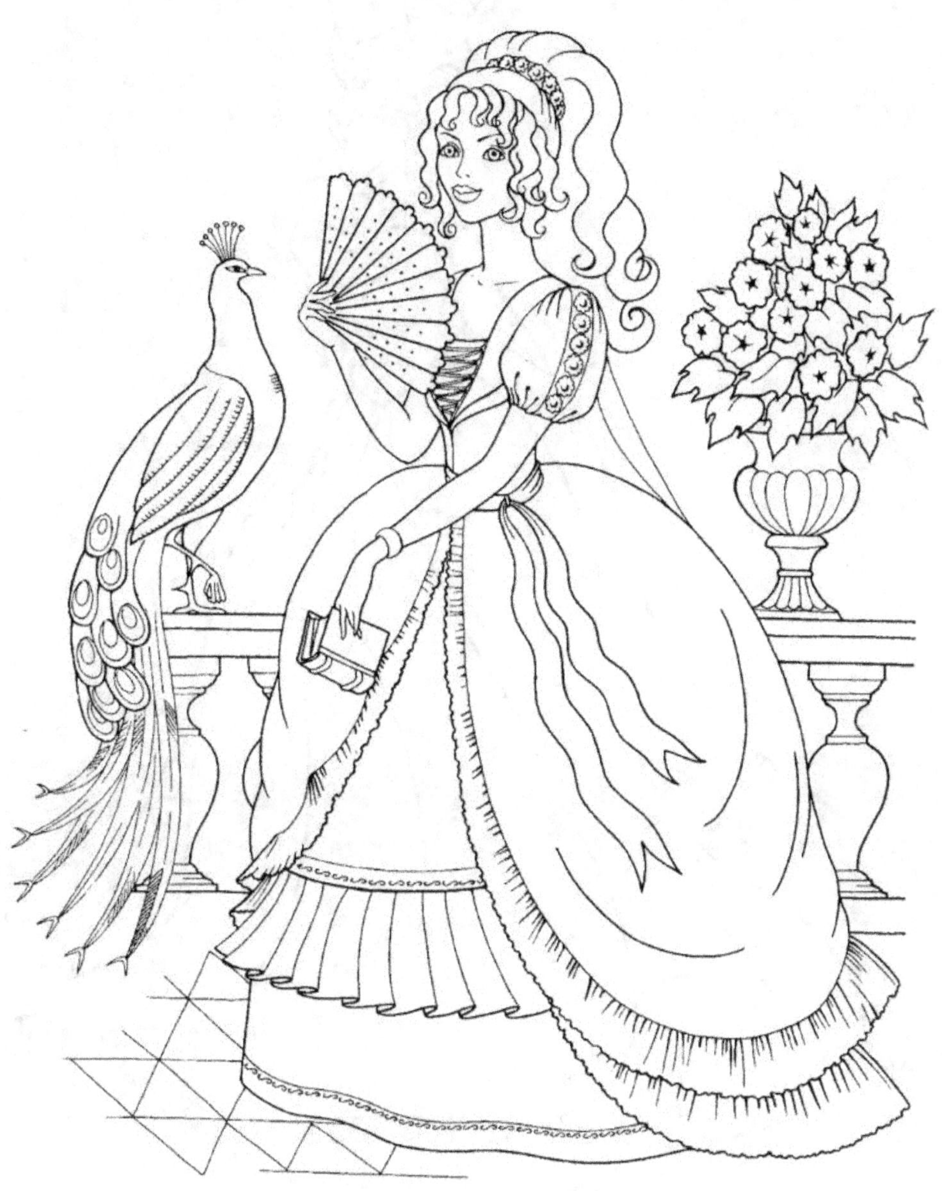

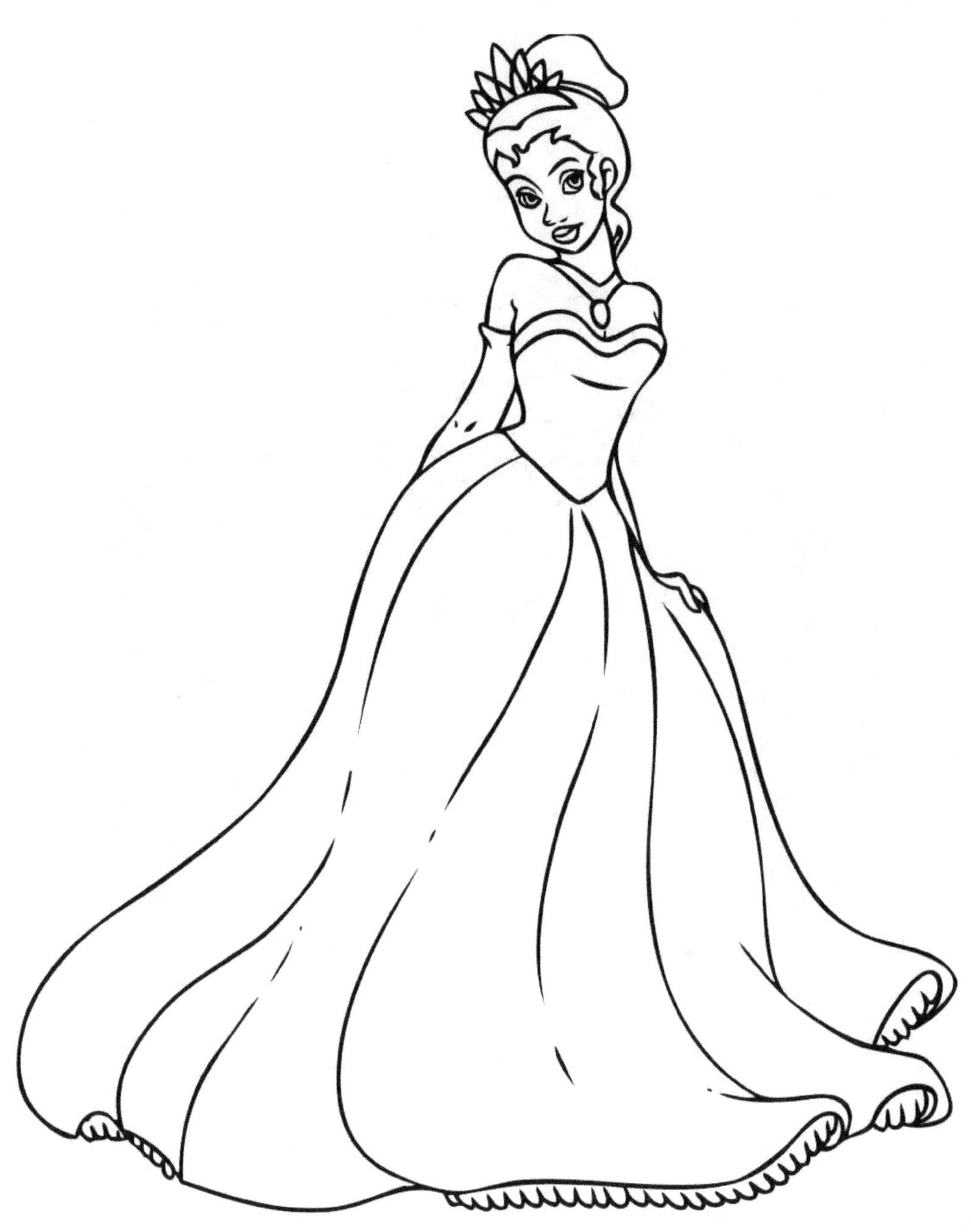

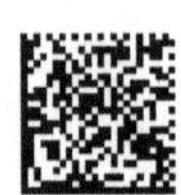